What makes French girls as serenely self-satisfied as purring cats . . . and catnip to the men who admire them?

We'd all be as free as the French girl if we looked like her, right? The stereotypical French girl is often insolently thin, casually chic, and fashionable despite a simple wardrobe. With or without makeup she is always put together and utterly self-confident, imbued with natural elegance and an elusive distance that is particularly, maddeningly French.

But this stereotype obscures delicious paradoxes about the French girl and her body. Yes, she does have an exasperating tendency to be thin. Reams have been written trying to decode the mystery of a people who smoke, drink, eat goose fat, and still look fabulous. But in reality, the French girl comes in a multitude of styles and body shapes, and whatever her figure, she looks remarkable and just plain sexy.

The French girl understands that sexy is a state of mind. Her relationship to food and her body is sensual, not tyrannical, and she takes pleasure in both.

—from *Entre Nous*

A Woman's Guide to
Finding Her Inner French Girl

Debra Ollivier

Entre Nous

St. Martin's Griffin   New York

A LARK PRODUCTION

www.stmartins.com

Illustrations by Michael Storrings

Design by Susan Walsh

Library of Congress Cataloging-in-Publication Data

Ollivier, Debra.
    Entre nous : a woman's guide to finding her inner French girl / Debra
Ollivier.
        p. cm.
    "A Lark production."
    ISBN 0-312-30876-0 (hc)
    ISBN 0-312-30877-9 (pbk)
    EAN 978-0132-30877-3
    1. Women—France. 2. Self-perception—France. 3. Beauty,
Personal—France. 4. Women—Clothing—France. 5. Women—
France—Sexual behavior. I. Title.

HQ1613 .0414 2003
305.4'0944—dc21
                                            2002037029

20 19 18 17 16 15 14 13

Contents

French habits and manners have their roots in a civilization so profoundly unlike ours—so much older, richer, more elaborate and firmly crystallized—that French customs necessarily differ from ours more than do those of more primitive races; and we must dig down to the deep faiths and principles from which every race draws its enduring life to find how like in fundamental things are the two people whose destinies have been so widely different.

—EDITH WHARTON, *French Ways and Their Meaning*

Preface

How to sum up in one book the particu-
larities and essential qualities of the French
girl? She is mythic and mysterious, she is
compelling and contradictory; she's part of a
legendary history that includes visionary
guerrilla milk maidens and ruthless queens.
She is, in short, a star in the pantheon of feminine beauty and strength, but if you tell her

all this she will laugh in disbelief. "How funny!" one French girlfriend said upon hearing how she is perceived outside of her country's little hexagon.

The French girl, of course, is a composite of many delicious paradoxes, and it is nearly impossible to sum her up. There is the bohemian who trolls Parisian flea markets and the intellectual who lives in books. There is the eternal student who flutters in the ether of France's grand universities and the iconoclast (and yes, while we're at it, the militant anti-American). There is the tomboy and the princess; the classic bourgeois and the stately matron; and the conservative rural mother who has only been to Paris once or twice in her life because, after all, it's stressful and confusing and life is just fine in her small town, *merci beaucoup*. And lest we forget, there is the first-generation French girl, whose North African and Asian roots bring a complex mélange into the somewhat staid underpinnings of the traditional culture. And all these types, of course, come in every possible body shape, size, and look.

Our own culture has taken generously from hers—we have everything from haute couture to haute cuisine, and even a racy vocabulary that made our own language blush back in the days of stuffy Victorian English. And yet when it comes to the French girl herself, we often fixate on the stereotype (you know her: the svelte Euro goddess in high heels) rather than the archetype. But it is in the archetypal French girl—the one who defies the stereotypes, the one whose essential, overarching qualities imbue her with that particularly alluring *je ne sais quoi*—that we find our true goddess in this tale.

The archetypal French girl is not the woman you see on the cover of fashion magazines or on the big screen. Nor is she the woman you see strolling the rue St. Honoré. She is a distillation of her culture's complex and enduring predilections: She is an essence, a way of being, a mind-set—and she exists in us all. She is that part of us that is free—and not bound up by the joyless strings of Puritan morality or guilt. She's that part of us that has a sense of continuity in life, that doesn't rush, that feels sexy for no apparent reason. She is, more fundamentally, that part of us that does not want to live according to what others think she should be. She is her own woman. Entirely.

Nearly a century ago, Edith Wharton lived in France and wrote essays that captured the spirit of the French with such clarity that they still ring true today. It is through her ageless wisdom and observations about the French girl that we consider how we might unstuff the suitcase of our emotional lives and fill it with something more meaningful; how we might have a life instead of just make a living; and finally, how we might trek through the wilderness of our own minds not to *be* French (because that's not the point), but to slow down, chuck the diet books, ignore the how-to manuals, stop the endless res-olutions, and get in touch with our inner French girls.

La Tête

As it happened, the first true French girl
I ever met was Natalie. She was living in an
old renovated farmhouse at the time, just
south of Paris, where her husband and a
group of aspiring Truffauts were shooting a
film on unrequited love and existentialism.
(Only in France, no?) Natalie was wearing a
close-fitting black skirt over a voluptuously

pregnant belly, a camisole under a sheer blouse, and suede ankle boots. Her long hair was pulled back with a tortoiseshell barrette, though several fugitive strands tumbled onto her shoulders in unruly wisps, and she wore not one bit of makeup.

She was perfectly content and undeniably sensual, and when she spoke, which she did sparingly, you could tell she had a superbly intelligent mind. It was just all there, that incredible mix of beauty and brains that seems to imbue French girls with such interesting faces, such refined strength. It would have been easy to suggest that Natalie's allure was a function of something physical (her hair, her clothes, her overall look). Too easy. Like so many French girls Natalie's *je ne sais quoi* was less about her look and much more about her history: She had been shaped by generations of independent feminine spirits (countless queens, courtesans, and traditional French mothers); by unspoken codes of social grace and courtly love; by a legacy of feminine guile and intellectual brawn—and at that moment, walking down a country lane in a land where the layers of civilization were so thick you could almost cut them with a knife, all I wanted to do was leave the planet and be reborn French.

That, alas, was not to be.

I did, however, have the opportunity to live long enough in France to ponder, with a certain privileged proximity, those essential qualities that make the French girl so French. And in coming to understand the core principles that shape her perception of the world, I began to wonder how we, with our own cultural baggage and American juju, could integrate some of these qualities into our own lives and get in touch with our own inner French girls. Clearly we had to look past the fabled French style—"the look," if you will, that it is so easy to mistake for the defining feature of the French girl—and consider the expression of something much deeper, some basic truths about how she sees herself and carries herself in the world.

If you peel back the surface details, these essential qualities emanate like spokes into every aspect of the French girl's life: They influence how she carries herself, the clothes she wears, the men she brings into her life (or doesn't). They shape her self-image, what she reads, how and what she eats. They temper her experience of sensuality, her notion of time, and the tenor of her family life.

Like the smooth surface of a river stone, many of these qualities have been honed by centuries of culture and civilization. Still, many of them can be cultivated (to each woman, her own private garden), and in the following chapters we'll explore how. For now, just what exactly are these essential qualities, and how do they shape the French girl's perception of herself and the world at large?

She Is Self-Possessed

If you strip away the stereotypes and contradictions about her, one of the fundamental qualities associated with the French girl is her sense of self-possession. She is entirely, unequivocally self-contained. She is focused on living her

For listening to the voices and following her heart. _La Pucelle_ (the maid) was honest and passionate and fearless—she really was the first guerrilla girl. We consider her short life of amazing accomplishment and we want to be better, believe harder, stand taller. See the 1928 classic silent film by Carl Dryer, _The Passion of Joan of Arc_, or the 1999 talkie, _The Messenger: The Story of Joan of Arc_ by Luc Bresson. Read scholar Regine Pernoud's _Joan of Arc: Her Story_ or Vita Sackville-West's somewhat flawed but beautifully written _Saint Joan of Arc_. Or better yet, read _Joan of Arc_, Mark Twain's (yes, that Mark Twain) meticulous and lovingly executed biographical novel. He considered this his most important and finest work. Don't tell Tom and Huck.

own full life, following her own agenda and cultivating her actual self, rather than reinventing herself or pining away to be someone she's not. Throughout her life, she invests herself in learning and experiencing, not to _change_ who she is, but to _become_ more fundamentally and more fully who she truly is. Taking her cues predominantly from within—from the life of her mind and the exercise of her critical intelligence—she is imbued with a strength of character and a certain sensitivity. Because she is sure of who she is on the inside, she naturally, inevitably, appears sure of herself on the outside.

There is also a lovely, dreamy paradox about the

French girl, and it's this: in having a strong sense of self, she's able to let go of herself; that in being self-contained, she's able to be vulnerable—all without unraveling at the seams. It's that mélange of sensitivity and *sang froid* that so delicately lingers around her, like a subtle aura.

Every choice she makes underscores this basic relationship to herself: The French girl tends to her personal, private garden with dedication. By taking care of herself in ways both large and small, she is free to take care of others, free to focus on real living rather than rushing through the essentials. She understands that being of service to others is contingent on being of service to oneself. There is nothing accidental here, nothing random in her composure: It is the result of an awareness of—and commitment to—herself.

She Seeks Sensuality

There is also something more corporeal at play here—an inspired sensuality, an exalted simplicity that intoxicates us Anglo-Saxons when we visit France—and that is the premium the French girl puts on experiencing pleasure: Pleasure in ordinary moments. Pleasure in extraordinary moments. She does not confuse commerce with culture and the narrative in her life does not come from what she buys or sees on TV; rather, it comes from getting sensual satisfaction in the moment, from feeling an almost tactile pleasure and evocative power in the seemingly mundane. Remember Audrey Tautou in *Amélie?* She dips her hands into sacks of grain just for the pleasure of how it feels. She relishes the crackle of a teaspoon breaking the crust of a crème brûlée. And she soothes herself skipping stones at Canal St. Martin.

Sensuality is so pervasive in her life that it is almost transparent. It is in the general texture of life, the patina of age that comes with time. It is in the baking of bread by hand, the aging of wine. It is in the color of inkwells or damask drapes, in the uproarious flamboyance of architecture. And it is fundamentally in the perfection of

"One is not born a woman; rather one becomes a woman."

SIMONE DE BEAUVOIR

imperfections—the complexity and realness that create character, depth, and charm.

Being anchored in these priorities gives the French girl the sophisticated and sexy self-confidence that has put her in the Feminine Hall of Fame and made her an icon worldwide. She so fully and unequivocally inhabits her own space, and with such individualistic flair, that it seems as if even from the earliest age she has always been sure of who she is and where she's going. And perhaps she has. As Edith Wharton saw her, ". . . she is, in nearly all re-

Le Film

LA DOUBLE VIE DE VERONIQUE
(The Double Life of Veronique)

See this for the luminous, rapturous performance of star Irene Jacobs as Veronique, who reminds us that if we're not living with a truly sensual appreciation of everything around us, we're not really living at all.

spects, as different as possible from the average American woman. The French woman is *grown-up*."

She Practices Discretion

From her sense of self-possession flows another essential quality that shapes her world definitively: discretion. The French girl wears her discretion like a filter or a screen, and every decision in her life passes through it: what she wears, how she spends her time, who she lets into her life, what she says (and does not say). Discretion is an ongoing act of self-editing.

The French girl understands that even the smallest gesture is a choice, a purposeful selection of one path over another, one outcome over another, one impression over another. There is nothing random or haphazard about her. Everything is about personal choice and behind every decision is a deliberate, thoughtful reflex: *Is this really me? Should I speak my mind or hold back? How should I approach this particular person? How much of myself do I reveal? What is the true value of this friendship, this experience, this thing? Does this make me feel good, sexy, alive?*

The French girl's discretion is often most apparent in what she chooses *not* to say. Like her culture she's private and nonconfessional. (We, on the other hand, are public and confessional. Sit two Americans on a park bench and you'll get at least one life story in five minutes flat.) By not revealing herself easily—her secrets, her inclinations, her inner life—she can sometimes appear self-centered. But in fact, what is often perceived as self-centered *chez la femme française* is actually the state of being centered on herself. And her distant allure is frequently the subtle glimmer of the exclusive world she keeps to herself.

History, with all its twisted tales, has taught the French girl that the intimate details in her world are a form of currency that she shouldn't just throw around. Being nonconfessional by nature, the French girl largely avoids the full wrath of the gossip trap: The chitting. The chatting. The feasting on morsels of other people's pathos. She also understands that when you give away pieces of your own life, they go back into the oven half-baked, only to get re-consumed by other thrill-seekers of gab in an all-you-can-eat buffet. On a small scale it wreaks havoc in lives. On a big scale, it turns personal tragedy into tabloid entertainment and trivializes powerful moments.

The French girl does gossip (she's human, after all) but her culture respects privacy in ways that stupefy Americans and she, too, takes on this guard. Her tendency is to mind her own business. To be discreet. To think before she speaks. And because she doesn't need vicarious pleasures or the approval of others to exist, she often appears as if she could not care less what you think of her. And in fact, she doesn't.

"From their freedom of view combined with their sensuous sensibility they have extracted the sensation they call 'Le plaisir,' which is something so much more definite and more evocative than what we mean when we speak of pleasure. 'Le plaisir' stands for the frankly permitted, the freely taken, delight of the senses, the direct enjoyment of the fruit of the tree called golden."
EDITH WHARTON

Le Livre

FRENCH WAYS AND THEIR MEANING
by Edith Wharton

It's no secret that Edith Wharton had a giant crush on the French. She lived in France for several years and had a front row seat on the workings of French culture. Despite certain dated notions, this little-known treasure of essays sheds the kind of light on the French—and especially French women—that only an astute observer and perceptive writer like Wharton could pull off.

The French girl is brought up to be polite, but she is not necessarily brought up to be a good girl. Lucky her—that Anglo-Saxon imperative to be liked (and *be* like everyone else) is not high on her list. Her culture exalts the iconoclast, the nonconformist, the artist and original thinker—all of which makes it more natural for her to say No to prevailing pressures. She is able to draw the line between who she is and who she is not on every level, so she is able to discriminate without ambivalence—whether it's about a skirt or a man that simply isn't right for her life. It also makes it easy for her to ignore the pressure to be all things to all people, and to appreciate the company of herself—with a book, a glass of wine—over the filler noise of other people who don't really rock her world.

This ability to say No—graciously, thoughtfully—reinforces her natural discretion: What she eventually *does* let into her life is more a reflection of herself—and by

"When I was growing up in the suburbs of Paris in the 60s and trying to figure out who I wanted to be, the essence of what it was to be a French woman seemed both obvious and elusive. It was not something you could buy via the right pair of shoes or pants or haircut—although those things definitely helped. It had to do with sexual self-confidence, and with a deep conviction that being a woman was different in every way from being a man. You recognized it immediately in some women—and not just in Paris and on the pages of *Marie Claire* and *Elle*, but even in tiny, obscure French provincial towns. . . . The essence of French femininity for me: brainy, erotic, self-confident and vulnerable, yet eminently in control."

CATHERINE TEXIER

default more authentic. Even in her impulses there's a certain intention, but she's not quick to jump on any bandwagons. Like the painter who knows the rules well enough to break them (and create an *oeuvre d'art*), the French girl knows conventions well enough to move beyond them. Which means that when all's said and done, her life ends up custom-made, not made by custom.

The Art of Saying No

Having discretion means never having to say you're sorry for saying No. It means being able to gracefully say No without remorse, guilt, or making excuses. It means not saying Yes when you really want to say No (then backpedaling your way into what you really want through white lies and entanglements).

The French girl has mastered the art of saying No by rejecting the "shoulds" that throw her off her personal path and waste her time. That includes advertising that lures her into the pastures of self-doubt and friends who drag in drama. (Are they really essential friends in the first place? As Bette Davis once said, "Yes, burn your bridges!") No (*non!*) is one of the most useful words in a French girl's vocabulary. Seize the moment or it will most definitely seize you.

She Takes Time

"I abhor the digital watch!" Chantale once exclaimed while glancing at a display case. "The analog watch is so much more human, with its hands going around the dial like the earth going around the sun. Did you know that digital time is measured by the 9,192,631,770 oscillations per second of a cesium atom?" (Frankly, I did not.) She sighed and rewound the tiny stem on her analog watch. "Who needs that kind of pressure?"

The French girl's notion of time is that of a *flâneur*—a

stroller, one who does not go places with a particular objective or precise schedule but allows the ambling course of general intentions to guide her into unplanned encounters and special unexpected pleasures. In her world, time is not money. Time is life. As Wharton once described it, real life is deep and complex and slowly developed, and has its roots in fundamental things. And you cannot experience those fundamental things, or true pleasure in life, without taking your time.

These fundamental things to which Wharton refers are the backbone of ritual, and by their very nature rituals are about time: They honor time. They take time. And they've existed over time (lifetimes, that is). We're not talking about grandiose or ceremonial rituals (though they can be either) but rather the countless small rituals that imbue ordinary life with pleasure and meaning: The family meal.

Borrow A Page From the French Girl's Book: Discretion

Think before you speak. Leave some things unsaid. Respect secrets. Consider your life your personal currency—and invest it wisely. Resist the impulse to turn over other people's stones. Cultivate the art of saying No with mindfulness. Make decisions from your own center. Be wary of shoulds. Exercise deliberateness in all decisions. Stay on the high road but make room for compassion. Bring unconventional wisdom into your life. Go gently against the grain.

An hour of uninterrupted solitude. The pilgrimage back home. The monthly evening out with an inner circle of friends.

Each small ritual involves an investment of time, and there is no greater return than the investment one makes in oneself. The French girl understands that time is immutable and that she, on the other hand, is not. By taking quality time for herself she's free to give it back to others. And because she puts her time into high-yield meaningful things, the return on her investment is not measured in monetary value or social gain but rather in the deeply satisfying pleasures of the moment.

This is not to say that the French girl has the patience of a monk. She does not. She sometimes drives like a bat out of hell, would park in your kitchen if she could find a

French Girls We Love
JEANNE MOREAU

For being a perfect combination of femininity and intelligence, sophistication and sensuality, heat and light. As rocker Patti Smith once said of Moreau, "She's so self-contained, she could start a forest fire. Anna Magnani was great. Piaf was great. But they were so much emotion. Jeanne Moreau, she's got brains. It's like she's got an intellect in her movement." Precisely. See Jeanne Moreau in Louis Malle's *Les Amants* (*The Lovers*), Truffaut's *Jules et Jim*, and Tony Richardson's *Mademoiselle*, for starters.

space, and cuts in line (a French speciality), but when it comes to the essential things in life—the personally relevant, the intimately clear—she does not rush. She does not force today what can get done tomorrow. Time is relative: life is short, memories are long. To all things a season, quite literally.

She Values Quality and Authenticity

My friend Frédérique embodies that very French principle of quality over quantity. She has an almost singular precision in the way she dresses (a closet full of just the right clothes), in what she owns (things with meaning, things that evoke memories), in all the things that inhabit her world. Even objects that are propped up against a corner or thrown onto the floor of her country home (a battered hoe, a pair of muddied, well-worn boots) have a certain particularity about them, as if they were each imbued with a soul. Less is truly more, as long as it's an expression of quality and authenticity. She resists the expendable, the disposable, the trendy, the *faux*. She knows that having too much choice does not necessarily give her more ways to define herself. She prefers the singular wild flower to the pre-made bouquet. The small car to the big machine. She invariably buys one perfect high-quality dress and not several less satisfying, on-sale ones. And she instinctively knows how to mix and match with natural creativity.

The French girl's preference for quality over quantity ties directly into her ability to say No: No to excess in people, things or ideas; No to what doesn't grace her world. Quality over quantity is not just about material things. Who inhabits her world, who feeds her mind, who's allowed into her private garden? The French girl would rather spend time alone than with people who simply fill a void. As Frédérique puts it, "Give me Proust or a good short story over idle chatter any time."

How to Shop Like a French Girl

It is impossible to shop American-style with Frédérique because instant gratification is not part of her gestalt. Neither are credit cards. If she can't afford it, she won't buy it. If it doesn't fit (or make her feel good, or flaunt what she's got), she won't wear it. If she can't find it, she won't compromise. If she loves it, she won't toss it. She reuses it, rethinks it, lets it age.

Like Frédérique, Anne is also influenced by the natural constraints of geography. "I shop mainly in the center of Paris," she says, "next door to my office or flat. I hate big stores and I have no car: I shop as I walk, which limits the quantity of my shopping as far as holding bags is concerned! If I'm on my way to a business meeting I might stumble upon a new pair of shoes, or a beautiful silver

"The beauty that addresses itself to the eyes is only the spell of the moment; the eye of the body is not always that of the soul."
GEORGE SAND

ring, or an old crystal bowl. Paris is full of unique opportunities, and to see them you really have to *live* in the city, not just speed through it on your way to somewhere else."

When the French girl shops, it isn't a solitary act of buying something new. It's part of a lifelong process of editing her environment, making small but meaningful additions or adjustments to her home, her closet, her life.

When you shop like a French girl, you buy only one of anything—and make sure it's the best quality you can afford. You know what you want and where to find it (and if you don't, you learn: You have your *carnet d'adresses* filled with details on special shops—where to buy those velveteen pants, that whimsical frock coat, those fetish shoes or the lofty Viennese hats. Where to find those private twice-a-year sales and exclusive, once-in-a-lifetime deals in unmarked loft warehouses, where the French girl's passion borders on frenzy). You update with accents that are both unique and timeless. Crimson linen napkins or vintage porcelain to use with your grandmother's old ivory tablecloth. A distinctive antique watch or flamboyant scarf to nuance your specific look. An Italian leather portfolio or South American satchel to carry to meetings. You invest in authentic things of quality that will endure and you focus on what's essential. And when you *do* find those essential things that work for you, you jump. "There is an antique shop I love on the rue Oberkampf," says Anne. "I look at the window every day, just a glance, and if something attracts me I buy it right then, otherwise I will miss it and regret it all my life!"

While you're sensitive to the winds of change, you're not prey to the whims and persuasions of every fad and ad. What's in or out is less important than what's you: your passions, your personal style.

She Cultivates Her Own History

One afternoon I stumbled into my friend Hélène, who was off in her high heels to march the streets in protest over threats to socialized medicine. "Inconvenient but imper-

Fine and Ordinary Things

The French girl understands that luxury is not about glamour. It's about beauty in ordinary life. It's about great power in small things. Proust had his madeleine. Colette had her pens. She also had a wealth of other writing accoutrements she described in loving detail:

"A pad of virgin blotting paper; an ebony ruler; one, two, four, six pencils, sharpened with a penknife and all of different colors; pens with medium nibs and fine nibs, pens with enormously broad nibs, drawing pens no thicker than a blackbird's quill; sealing wax, red, green and violet; a hand blotter, a bottle of liquid glue, not to mention slabs of transparent amber-colored stuff known as 'mouth glue'; the minute remains of a spahi's cloak reduced to the dimensions of a pen wiper with scalloped edges; a big inkpot flanked by a small inkpot, both in bronze, and a lacquer bowl filled with a golden powder to dry the wet page; another bowl containing sealing wafers of all colors (I used to eat the white ones); to right and left of the table, reams of paper, cream-laid, ruled, watermarked."

ative!" she shouted as she waved me off on her way to the metro, brandishing a handmade banner.

The French girl's inner strength and her sense of self-possession are honed by a relationship to history: not just her own personal history, with its peaks and valleys, its particular geography; but also to her culture's collective history. She has two thousand years of history at her doorstep, for starters, and reminders on almost every street that heads literally rolled down the cobblestones in bloody revolution against the hubris of royalty. The value of memory and political engagement is passed down at a young age, and she carries it into her adult life.

And so the French girl is a political animal in the best sense. She has a long memory and an unwavering appreciation for hard-won privileges and a drive to maintain them: Her rights, her children's rights, human rights . . . The French girl has conviction and opinions and she expresses them wholeheartedly in the streets, high heels and all. Says Hélène, "There is nothing more unfashionable than political apathy."

Fin

Ironically, over the years Natalie, this complex and intelligent woman, would teach me the enduring truths behind certain clichés. Like beauty is more than skin deep. Think before you speak. Don't wear your heart on your shirtsleeve. Be true to yourself.

On many occasions I'd watch Natalie dismiss the images in fashion magazines ("Fairy tales!" she'd laugh, looking a little bit like a lustrous Snow White herself), read voraciously, excuse herself in the middle of an event to take a little nap "because I feel I must," and wear the same three things in hip and varying combinations over the

French Girls We Love

SIMONE DE BEAUVOIR

For turning the lights on with *The Second Sex* and for giving Jean-Paul Sartre a run for his money. Philosopher, novelist, essayist—Simone de Beauvoir is known as one of the twentieth century's most interesting and important women. Her memoirs reveal an independent, self-defined woman who made conscious (if existentialist!) choices regarding love and work, her path as an intellectual and a writer, and of a lifestyle informed by brutal honesty and complete freedom. She was unapologetically committed to Sartre, who by all accounts was no picnic of a life's companion, and even chose to be buried in the same grave. We love that kind of love and we love her fierce individualism. Read *The Second Sex*, of course, as well as her first novel, *L'Invitée*, a fictionalized account of one of Sartre's early affairs. In it, the motto of the protagonists, who represent de Beauvoir and Sartre, is: "You and I are simply one. Neither of us can be described without the other."

course of several days. I watched her eat with a certain lustful, guilt-free pleasure, refuse to wear a watch, and get passionate about politics or about simply being alone. I admired the fact that she could hold her alcohol (lots of it), make a great quiche with half a cup of flour and one egg, and speak Latin because "it's beautiful, and why not?" To say that Natalie was self-possessed is an understatement: She lived her life willfully but mindfully and one day, without realizing it, she summed up her French girlishness in one single line: "If you stay true to yourself, you will always remain on track, even if that track takes you off the beaten path, to places you could not possibly imagine."

Two

Le Corps

The first time I went to the Riviera, capi-
tal of continental, laissez-faire beach culture,
my French friend, Francine, did what all
the natives did with simple abandon: She
whipped off her bikini top (what else did I
expect her to do?) and stretched out on the
bright, rocky beach with her breasts saluting
the sun. I, on the other hand, didn't even own

a bikini at the time—just a practical one-piece and some bulky American body-image baggage. While my topless friend lounged oblivious to the gawking stares of Anglo-Saxon tourists, I wondered with both envy and admiration: How does she let herself go with such natural ease?

Well, we'd all be as free as the French girl if we looked like her, right? The stereotypical French girl is often insolently thin, casually chic, and fashionable despite a simple wardrobe. With or without makeup she is always put together and utterly self-confident, imbued with natural elegance and an elusive distance that is particularly, maddeningly French.

But this stereotype obscures delicious paradoxes about the French girl and her body. Yes, she *does* have an exasperating tendency to be thin. Reams have been written trying to decode the mystery of a people who smoke, drink, eat goose fat, and still look fabulous. (Hint: It's not about diets.) And yes, there *is* pressure to be thin in France, which may explain why if you're a size twelve or bigger, good luck finding clothes in a French boutique. But in reality, the French girl comes in a multitude of styles and body shapes, and whatever her figure, she looks remarkable and just plain sexy.

The French girl understands that sexy is a state of mind. Her relationship to food and her body is sensual, not tyrannical, and she takes pleasure in both. (This may explain why the French are often preoccupied with food and sex, and Anglo-Saxons with work and money.) A certain

Le Film

TROP BELLE POUR TOI
(Too Beautiful For You)

This is a film only the French could have made. Married to a woman who embodies the ultimate French beauty (played by model Carole Bouquet), Bernard (Gérard Depardieu) falls passionately in love with his secretary, Colette. Colette is the opposite of Bernard's wife—she's ordinary, a little frumpy, and plump. But Bernard is attracted to something intensely real in Colette. Says Colette with a certain pride, "I know I'm plain but I've always felt free: in my body, in my head. I'm a woman who is alive."

universal truth prevails for her, which my luscious, curvaceous friend Nadine explains this way: "Men love flesh. They're hard-wired for it. French women know this and they're knock-outs even with a little bit of extra belly or butt. We're not out there exercising like crazy, we're enjoying life as it is."

Unlike her American *cousines*, rather than camouflage herself in a hip-hiding tunic, the French girl flaunts what she's got—curves, belly and all. And if she's uncomfortable with her body, chances are high she won't go on a Draconian diet and broadcast her calorie counting and weight loss for all the world to hear. She'll quietly modify the way she eats and work on her body without fanfare. And while there *is* pressure to stay trim in her world (obesity ranks high on the list of things the French love to hate, along with taxes and other signs of unacceptable excess), weight is a private matter—it's her business and not an enlightened topic of conversation. Which is why you're more likely to hear French girlfriends discussing the philosophical underpinnings of the latest arthouse film rather than the respective merits of Atkins or the Zone.

Growing Up Sexy

It wasn't until I had my first child in France that I understood the more subtle and pervasive influences on the young French girl's mind. Like the fact that her perception of her body is not shaked and baked in the hellfires of Puritanism (she's Latin, remember?). Or that she does not grow up with a single standard of beauty. Or that she does not have Barbie for a national beauty queen.

The French girl grows up with an almost rapturous cultural appreciation for the human form—not just exalted on museum walls but in daily life, everywhere, in a multitude of little details—and a matter-of-factness about the body that shapes her perception of herself in the most fundamental ways. She grows up playing with anatomically correct dolls (even with anatomically correct, intact boy dolls. A replica of the real thing! *Et pourquoi pas?*). Some French public swimming pools have coed changing rooms, which don't inspire displays of public nudity but rather a certain detached curiosity and nonchalance. And tactile physical contact is part of the French experience

French Girls We Love

MARIANNE

For being the fearless, shirtless symbol of the French republic itself. She's invariably depicted on everything from national currency to school textbooks with her patriotic, freewheeling breasts exposed. While Marianne is most famously depicted as Delacroix's *Liberté*, a number of celebrity French *femmes* have represented her over the years, including Brigitte Bardot and Catherine Deneuve. Top model Laetitia Casta was recently voted to depict Marianne because (in the words of one French mayor) "She obviously has the nicest bust of all." Casta, who once declared that her breasts were raised on butter and crème fraîche, was thrilled to represent this treasured national icon. "To represent France, liberty and a certain idea of what a woman is," she said, "that's a hell of a responsibility." (No kidding!)

on the most basic level: The ordinary French greeting, of course, is a fleeting moment of physical intimacy in the form of two kisses, and sometimes four. (And when it comes to kisses, first-grader Jean-Michel can peck classmate Claudette on the mouth without getting kicked out of school. "This is natural for children," explained the director of our son's school. "If you forbid them from doing what is natural, they will seek it out later in ways that are unnatural and perverse.")

The Naked Truth

There is in France a kind of collective, cultural shrug about nakedness. Take my first French gynecological exam. My gynecologist's office was in a lavish eighteenth-century manor house in the heart of the Marais (such is the particular charm of living in France). A trim, officious woman, the doctor sat me down and, after a few minutes of discussion, asked me to disrobe and lie down on the table. "The table?" I asked. "*Oui*," she replied, pointing to an examining table that I hadn't noticed at the far end of her office, "*la table*."

"*La table*" looked awfully barren to me. Where was the separate changing room? Where was the little hook for my clothes? Where was the little paper gown to cover my body? Where were the dog-earred, dated issues of *Good Housekeeping* and *Self* magazine that I could read to keep my mind off the fact that I would soon be naked and mer-

French Girls We Love

JOSEPHINE BAKER

For her uninhibited sensuality as a performer and a woman. Famous for wearing nothing more than a skirt made of feathers or bananas on the Paris stage, she was one of the most photographed, talked about, and admired women in the world. An American by birth and a French girl at heart, she found France to be the only place she could be the *individualiste* she truly was. She loved France, and France loved her right back. Listen to *Bonsoir, My Love*, watch HBO's *The Josephine Baker Story*, and read *Josephine: The Hungry Heart* by Jean-Claude Baker and Chris Chase.

cilessly exposed to the imminent pokings and probings of *le docteur*? "You mean just get naked right here, right now, in this room?" I asked. "Yes, Madame," she replied, "is there a problem?" (Well, I felt like saying, where do I start?)

It is all this basic business of the body, gloriously free from self-consciousness, delightfully accepting of nature's unruly ways, and unapologetically matter-of-fact, that actually primes the French girl to be more relaxed about her body from the get-go. Ditto for a cultural predilection for sensuality in all its forms—and for the strong sense that she owns her own body, whatever its shape. And this breeds what we Anglo-Saxons might perceive as curious contradictions: The French girl might wax her legs to perfection, for example, but let her armpit hair grow. (Says Nadine: "Legs are public, underarms are private, and men love them both, hair or no hair.") And she'll proudly walk around naked because she's free in her mind and thus—logically, obviously, by all French empirical standards—free in her body. And if you consider the staggering number of American women who are unhappy with their

"As soon as you notice your first wrinkle and your first white hair, sigh with ease. You are well on your way to becoming who you always wanted to be."
VÉRONIQUE VIENNE

bodies (a number that increases every year), that alone is something to ponder.

French journalist Christophe, who's had many amorous experiences on both sides of the Atlantic, sums it up this way: "French women are more comfortable being naked than American women. Even if they have physical imperfections. I've been with American women who were wild in bed, but when the lovemaking was over they'd cover up their bodies with a T-shirt or robe to go to the bathroom. French women don't do that. They just get up, entirely naked, and walk around."

Le Film

8 FEMMES
(Eight Women)

This movie will never be called a French classic—it's an odd sort of musical mystery farce—but it's a who's who of working French actresses that showcases the considerable grace and style of some pretty fabulous French girls. Catherine Deneuve, Isabelle Huppert, Fanny Ardant, Danielle Darrieux, Virginie Ledoyen, Emmanuelle Béart. These actresses are classic femmes fatales, and the style of each woman at her varying ages and stages of life is a lesson in itself.

Sound familiar? The specter of Puritanism may have left its paw prints on the American girl's body, but so, too, has the currency of sex. The resulting challenge: How to be a wholesome soccer mom and a vampish Victoria's Secret model at the same time? Topping off this layer cake of cultural contradictions are the unattainable super-model beauty stereotypes that have the American girl struggling with her weight and body image her entire life.

This is not to say that the French aren't concerned about their weight (*au contraire*) or that they don't use sex to sell just about everything (French advertising makes that abundantly clear); it's that they are Latin, they are sensualists, they embrace the female form in all its fleshy diversity. The French girl might be as thin as a twig or as voluptuous as Venus. She might have full hips, wide haunches. It doesn't matter. Where the American girl uses clothes to conceal and feels mercilessly exposed without them, the French girl flaunts her form and is the same person whether fully dressed or buck naked.

On Exercise

The distinctly American aesthetics of sports—the hard bodies, the gear, the redemption of blood, sweat, and tears on the treadmill—has no real place in the French girl's world. (Anything that requires too much work for too little pleasure is suspect in the eyes of the French.) In recent years it is fashion—the gentrification of the ungainly American tennis shoe, for example, and the hipness of well-being—that has made exercise slightly more palatable to the French, and inspired a modest percentage of Parisians to take to the streets toting gym bags and spandex.

Essentially, exercise in France enjoys nothing close to the evangelical status it does in the States, and the general pressure to look like a female triathlete simply does not exist. "Why do women want to have washer board stomachs and hard men's bodies?" Corinne asked me one day as she flew down the rue de Rivoli. We were on the way into the metro, and I was trying to pry out of her the secret to her own personal exercise regime. Of course, she had no secret. "I eat, I drink. I smoke. And then I walk very, very fast every day to and from this metro in my heels," she said above the din of the Château de Vincennes-La Défense metro line. "That is my secret!"

> ### Borrow a Page from The French Girl's Book: Body Love
>
> Get rid of the diet books. Get to know your body. Spend time on yourself. Get naked. Sleep naked. Dance naked. Skinny dip. Don't wear underwear. Love your body and your children will grow up loving theirs. Be realistic. Take the time to own your body: If you seek change, modify your relationship to food with patience and simplicity. Relax and enjoy the ride.

Vintage Sensuality

Of all the women who personify the quintessential French woman it's Catherine Deneuve who is queen—not so much for her classical beauty and her rarefied natural perfection, but rather, for becoming the modern incarnation of the sexy older woman. We've watched her age with an uncompromising possession of self, a certain ripening of the sensual faculties. She has become less porcelain and untouchable with age, and remarkably more sexy.

There are thousands of other incarnations of the same sexy older French woman. They are completely self-contained and stylish. Rather than chase after the fountain of youth, they claim with fierce independence the accrued wisdom of their years. They might wear their gray hair bundled in an elegant heap above their heads

A Visit to the Inner Beauty Salon

Style, beauty, sex appeal—the French girl understands that her self-image is a reflection of her inner life. If you're a French girl, how do you cultivate your inner beauty so that it shines through?

You seek beauty and sensuality everywhere. When you are fully conscious of beauty in the details of everyday life, this awareness is naturally reflected in your face and your way of being.

You feed your mind: You read. You make art. You cultivate opinions.

You express empathy. This involves living with a deep sense of passion and compassion—and it rewards you by bringing to life the truly human side of your nature.

You don't let anger or worry linger. You don't rush. Rather, you let go of hanging on to being all things to all people (and leaving little for yourself). You process your feelings so they don't take up permanent residence on your face.

You are game. You stretch your own boundaries of experience so that your sense of adventure is alive.

You nap. Because napping is more delicious than sleeping, and its undeniable pleasures will always reflect well on you.

or cut fashionably short. When you see one of them strolling the rue des Francs-Bourgeois or sipping an espresso in a local café, you invariably think: Please let me be like her when I get older.

Because the French girl moves through life as a grown-up, when she's *really* all grown up she's reached the pinnacle of a certain worldly authority. She has secrets. Things to teach. She does not reach that special place, by the way, until she's no longer green with youth and striving but flush with life experience. And that life experience gives her the strength to accept (and even wholeheartedly engage in) the discreet indiscretions we so often associate with the French! "We're less afraid of getting older," says Frédérique. "I'm not sure why. The French woman has her face-lifts and so on, but she's fundamentally less afraid of getting older and more accepting of age. I can't tell you why. That's just how it is."

La Liberté

Certainly this personal freedom is partly what gives the French girl her astonishing character and distinctive beauty. She's not self-conscious about her body, and she's free from any pressure to bend to a trend.

Absolute singularity *à la française* is as much about personal style as it is about a certain mindset. Thanks to her Latin sensibility, she maintains an unabashed commitment to her femininity that sets her apart from other modern women: It informs her innate style choices, and puts her on a lifelong path of self-care that begins, at a very young age, with religious care for her skin.

Skin and Sanctuary

Arguably, the French girl has the most pristine and practical relationship to her skin. Pristine because she grows
up surrounded by the most exclusive, highest quality
beauty care products in the world. Practical because she
grows up tending to her skin with stubborn regularity:
cleansing, steaming, peeling, scrubbing with dutiful care.
There's an *Institut de Beauté* on just about every corner
in Paris and on any given day you'll find the French girl
having her regular "*soin*" (facial or body care treatment).
"You have to go to the dentist on a regular basis," explains
Nadine. "You have to tune up your car. So why wouldn't
you do the same for your skin and body? It's not about
luxury. It's about maintenance."

Once again the French girl has history on her side: Take
away the stellar French names in beauty care and most
cosmetic counters would be bare. The French girl grows

What's On Her Vanity

Because her approach to beauty begins with skin care, she'll start with the best she can afford—and always with an eye for the virtues of simplicity and quality. Sisley. Lancôme. Yon Ka. For the budget-conscious, the high end of L'Oréal. She'll have a day cream, eye cream, and night moisturizer. Gentle facial cleanser and toner for the face. She has a natural bristle brush. One or two high-quality lipsticks (a fire engine red and a great neutral like soft brown or pinky peach), a light powder and powder blush, top-drawer mascara and eyeliner. The lightest pink or beige nail polish, and perhaps a real red for special occasions. For perfume, she has a couple of signature scents—one for cold weather, one for warm. Perhaps Chanel's *Cristalle* or Annick Goutal's *Eau d'Hadrien* for spring and summer, *Coco* (Chanel) for winter and fall. Because she's irrepressibly brand loyal, she might stick to her streamlined collection of skincare products for years.

up enjoying the physical and emotional value of unfettered, ritualized body care, and her well-being is ingrained in the fabric of French culture.

The French girl has an almost genetic predisposition to take care of herself. Because she grows up doing more with less, she's learned to make her bathroom (which is probably the size of your pantry closet) into a sacred space. Her bathroom is not just utilitarian; it's an expression of her personal aesthetic—a collection of antique perfume bottles might share shelf space with ornate baskets, luminous tubes of lipstick, Japanese powder brushes, and fine soaps. She might paint her bathroom gold with cobalt blue trim. It's a personal oasis, a little shrine that compels her body to linger. She devotes herself to this private, self-care time with a conviction that borders on religious: No interruptions. (*Au revoir, les enfants. Au revoir, mon mari.*) No phone. No excuses.

Borrow A Page from the French Girl's Book: Body Care

Invest in the care of your body. Put together a private stash of your favorite body care products and commit to a regular weekly hour of total solace. Pay attention to every part of your body, particularly your hands and feet. Feed your skin. Drink water. Indulge in sleep. Get massaged. Breathe deeply. Oxygenate your body and soul. Thank your body for its life force. Remember that to embrace sensuality as a human being you must be human with your body.

Makeup and Scent

The French have powdered and puffed themselves with extravagant flourish for centuries, but the distinguishing characteristic of the French girl's makeup is that it's often not distinguishable at all. *Au naturel* is her preference.

She invariably chooses quality over quantity and if it works, she doesn't mess with it. She uses makeup to conceal imperfections with the lightest touch (a silky translucent foundation, a fine powder) but never to camouflage her face or paint an entirely new one—and no fancy fingernails or overly coiffed hair, *s'il vous plaît*. She's subtle yet natural—so natural that if she suddenly has to run out the door without makeup, she doesn't feel naked.

Aromatique: The Short Story of French Scent

Every ancient culture has used aromatherapy in one form or another, but the French brought a method to the madness—and coined the term aromatherapy. French kings and queens indulged their olfactory senses in the most extravagant ways: Charles VIII worshipped perfume. Diane de Poitiers attributed her youthful appearance to copious amounts of fragrance and secret beauty water. Catherine de Médicis wore scented gloves and had special jewelry designed to contain poisonous aromatic potions. Her compatriots used scent on everything from their dogs and parrots to furniture, ribbons, hair, fans, and masks. They cultivated endless fields of flowers to pursue the ephemeral but intoxicating powers of perfume.

Later, when perfume went from the exclusive domain of royalty to regular use by the masses, Jean Patou decided to invent a perfume to combat the cynicism of his

time. He introduced Joy in 1930, and it became one of the
most successful and expensive perfumes in the world. The
rest, of course, is history.

The first French person I ever met who revered perfume was the aunt of a good friend who lived just down
the street. I was an impressionable young seven-year-old
very American girl at the time, and everything about this
woman seemed exotic; even her car was somehow sexy
(it was a low-slung, street-hugging Citroen).

Here was a woman who didn't make chocolate chip
cookies (instead, she baked soufflés) or peanut butter and
jelly sandwiches ("peanut *what*?" she once asked). She
wore her hair in a large complicated bun that seemed like
it might, with a little breeze, unravel into a heap of voluptuous curls (it never did). She ate dinner at a red velvet
restaurant called "Roberts" (which she pronounced "Roh-
BEAR"). She walked to football fields and grocery stores

On Hair

The French have been obsessed with hair over the centuries, experimenting with eccentric bouffants that involved coiled plaits, plucked hairlines, barbed hoops, hairpins, wooden rolls, onionskin dyes, oak paste, powdered wigs, dusted chignons, lace caps, feathers, beads, bows, baubles, gold nets, and rosettes. By the eighteenth century, courtly women spent hours having starch-dusted coiffures built over three-foot high wire cages and horsehair pads, and adorned them with ornate menageries that towered over their heads like wedding cakes. (In 1769, former baker and court hairdresser Legros de Rumigny put some order to the hair-raising madness by opening the first *Académie de la Coiffure*.)

Perhaps the hair follies of the past are at the root of a predilection for the *au naturel*, for even the French girl who spends hours a week with her *coiffeur* will leave with a look that is easy, simply tousseled or pixie-short. "American women change their look more often than French girls; they go to more extremes with their hair, are more open to risk," says Arnaud, an artist/hair designer who has coiffed women on both sides of the Atlantic and owns the ultra-hip Parisian salon, Headscape, in the Marais. "The French girl is more traditional. She tends to find the look that works for her and sticks with it."

in fancy little high heels (stunningly feminine, in the eyes of a seven-year-old). And she always wore Shalimar, which followed her in an aromatic cloud of heady amber, resin, and sweet musky notes.

It was all of these things—but particularly the Shalimar—that forged in my young mind a sense of the scent of a French woman. All French girls must love perfume, I decided at that age, and indeed most of them do—though they don't necessarily click along grocery aisles in high heels, and when it comes to scent they are more likely to take their cues from Marilyn Monroe. When asked what she wore to bed she replied, "Chanel No. 5."

The Look

One of the favorite mottoes of the French is "*On est individualiste!*" ("We are individualistic!"), which they often employ to justify their legendary intransigence. But nowhere is being "*individualiste*" more apparent than in the

French Girls We Love
AUDREY TAUTOU

For the irresistible smile that plays at the corners of her mouth, for her vintage Frenchness, for her thoroughly modern Frenchness, for her signature cropped bangs and for making flat shoes chic again. See *Amélie*, of course, but also see *Venus Beauté Institut* and *Happenstance*, two larkish romantic comedies.

way they dress. The French girl's personal style is rooted in a defiant sense of individuality and a true sense of self.

This sense of style is gleaned from girlfriends, from mothers, from women around her and from the culture at large. The same quest for originality that united haute couturier Jean-Paul Gaultier with discount bazaar Tati characterizes the inimitable sense of creativity in the French—to see in the ordinary a flash of the extraordinary; to transform the usual into the unusual.

"We French aren't the most attractive people on Earth when you really think about it," says Frédérique, "but we are perhaps the most obsessed with aesthetics. We know how to make ourselves look interesting, different. We know how to make the best of what we've got. We get inspiration from brands and fashion magazines—and we thoroughly love all things Italian: clothes, leather goods, furniture—but the idea is not to imitate but rather to use them as a point of departure, as a source of ideas to help cultivate a unique, personal look."

For the French girl clothes are a language, a personal vernacular. She doesn't dress to the trend, she dresses to her strengths and bends the trend (if it interests her) only to complement those strengths.

When it comes to the French girl's personal style, the first place to look is in her closet. We Americans grow up with closets the size of most Parisian bedrooms: we have walk-in closets, custom-made closets, wall-to-wall closets. The French, on the other hand, simply have water closets

The Perfect Black Dress

The French girl knows she'll wear this dress a thousand times before she dies—and she falls in love with it again every time she wears it. What puts the "perfect" in her perfect black dress?

This dress loves only her. From whatever angle she observes herself in the mirror, it makes the most of everything about her. One woman's perfect black dress is not another woman's perfect black dress, and therein lies the magic.

This dress plays many roles. She'll wear it with silk stockings and her finest jewelry to a formal affair; with an elegant jacket to an important engagement; with strappy sandals to a cocktail party; and with pearls and a hat to a funeral, to name a few places her black dress takes her.

Like everything else that's truly French, the perfect black dress is discreet. It does not give away too much about her; it provides a beautiful frame around the picture of her, but reveals none of her secrets. Therefore, it's not too short nor too low-cut, not too *avant garde* nor too old school, not too busy or too plain, and does not suggest you paid too much or too little for it.

(not the same thing). To offset this dramatic domestic inconvenience, the French use their stately armoires, and the sense of limited space has absolutely contributed to the French girl's relationship with clothes.

Where we Americans buy in volume and in blow-out bargain basement sales, the French are highly selective. Never mind the closet problem, the French girl understands that she only needs a few high-quality items and careful accents to reflect her unique sensibility.

That's why the French school of fashion advocates having those few perfect items: The perfect black dress. The perfect white blouse. The perfect pullover. The perfect overcoat. The idea here is singularity: pieces purchased one by one that slowly build up a quality wardrobe through discretion. A closet with a few quality items is worth much more than a wardrobe of so-so clothes—and (God forbid!) outfits. I once went vintage shopping with a French girlfriend and tried on a matching shirt and skirt. "Ah, no!" she reproached me. "You can't buy that! It matches too well!"

The French girl is generally understated, not overstated. She takes the time—even if it's just one extra minute—to stop and consider not only how she looks in her clothes but how she *feels* in them. She's built her wardrobe piece by piece, always with quality in mind (never quantity), so when she *does* just throw something on, it doesn't matter what she throws. It's all still part of an eclectic look. And all the pieces work for her and work together—no throwing open her armoire in the morning with a panicked, "*Mon Dieu!* What am I going to wear?"

In the most practical terms, this saves her time and gives her an ongoing—lifelong!—peace of mind about her look.

Whatever she pulls on naturally hangs together because she's chosen everything in her closet with her trademark discretion. Which is why she'd rather wear the same

Underneath It All

Victoria's little secret is Claudette's basic staple. French lingerie may be a wicked little luxury to some or an over-the-top luxury to others, but for many French girls it's *de rigueur*. She buys it for herself because it feels good and it looks good.

As with all things, she invests in quality: Chantel. La Perla. Eres. She loves real lace, pure cotton, fine silk—in a variety of colors, not just black and white. She has an almost genetic aversion to panty lines and would rather wear a thong—or no underwear at all—than be caught with a little embossed crescent riding up her half-moons. She owns several perfect alluring bras (the implications of cleavage are omnipresent here), one strapless, *bien sûr*, and fine hosiery, including sheer black seamed stockings. She also buys everyday stockings from discount bazaars like Tati ("because you go through stockings like water"). She might have one or two Petit Bateau items, but she usually buys Bateau more for her kids. If it strikes her personal fancy, she'll own a racy bustier or a whimsically sexy garter. And if anything starts to wear out—the elastic goes south, the runs keep running—she carefully reinvests in her collection of intimates. She often hand washes her modest quantity of lingerie with care (no drawer full of Jockeys waiting to take a beating in the washing machine). Her fine lingerie lasts, as well as her interest in wearing it, throughout her life.

dress three days in a row if it works for her, than three different things that just don't feel right. Quality, quality, quality . . . never quantity.

On Comfort

"I base most of my fashion taste on what doesn't itch," Gilda Radner once declared, pretty much summing up the American sense of fashion. As the French see it, the mar-

French Girls We Love
MARGUERITE DURAS

For living an extraordinary life and pouring it into highly acclaimed works such as *India Song*, a film she directed and which won France's Cinema Academy Grand Prize; *Hiroshima, Mon Amour*, a film for which she wrote the script and received an Academy Award nomination; and *The Lover*, the 1984 international bestseller that earned her the Goncourt, France's most prestigious literary prize. We love Duras for her exquisite prose, keen intelligence, and French-girl fashion statements: "For fifteen years I've had a uniform . . . black cardigan, straight skirt, polo-neck sweater and short boots in winter . . . A uniform is an attempt to reconcile form and content, to match what you think you look like with what you'd like to look like, what you think you are with what you want to suggest. You find this match without really looking for it. And once it's found it's permanent." Read her novels *The Sea Wall* and *The Lover*.

What's In Her Dream Closet

If money were no object, (and avoiding department stores because "we get lost in them and end up buying what we don't really need") what would the French girl have in her closet?

A classic suit and coat from Ventillo and Cacharel, a typical French brand that's experiencing a sort of rebirth these days.

Lots of superb pure wool Italian pullovers and one or two cashmere sweaters. And very little logo action. ("That is very 'down,' " says Anne, "the logos, the 'total look.' ") Perfect-fitting pants and long skirts from Joseph, all in black, and a pair of jeans by Marithé and François Girbaud.

Excellent quality T-shirts in a suitable variety of cuts and colors, perhaps Swiss—or the Gap!

One or two hip skirts from Scooter. Maybe one hippie-chic piece from Bisou-Bisou or a simple dress from Agnès B.

One great silk shirt and some simple cotton shirts, preferably in black.

One or two perfect black dresses ("Never, ever white!").

Two great hats and lots of scarves, one of which must be a Kenzo. Costume jewelry from anywhere eccentric for a touch of fantasy; maybe one great piece from Clio Blue. Maybe an old Hermès scarf inherited from childhood ("one with horses, travel . . .").

One beautiful black wool coat and one raincoat, preferably *not* in black to boost the spirit when it rains too much. One

Continued on next page . . .

very elegant and sporty Ramosport coat. (Ramosport began designing military coats more than a century ago. Today it's high-end design.)

One pair of boots by Tod's or Clergerie.

One pair of walking shoes by Prada ("preferably on sale!") or Camper (among the only Spanish brands known in France) for stomping through the city. Also one pair of DKNY tennis shoes ("All the rage among Parisians these days") and one pair of Stephan Kelian dress shoes ("I bought one pair ten years ago and they will never, ever be out of style. All of the shoes should be black, by the way, except one pair of red walking shoes or gold DKNYs").

A Longchamps or Coach handbag, also preferably on sale. Maybe Hermès or Vuitton "but better for inspiration, otherwise too showy and ridiculously overpriced." Also, a Just Campagne bag in soft leather.

The French girl will also have in her closet something very eccentric and kitschy that she bought for a one-night-only party, from Guerisold (Guerisold is a low-end but fun/funky style discount store) or the flea market, and something very high-end from L'Éclaireur for that one ultra-elegant soirée. Also for a party: One sexy pullover, preferably in black, a nice trouser with very feminine shoes (". . . the kind that make you miss the bus because you can't run in them!").

Plus a collection of unique vintage pieces that take an exceptionally long time and a good eye to find.

What She Might Have Kept Since Childhood

A Moroccan bracelet from her first trip as a young adult. Chipped Limoges dishes. A rolling pin and hair clips from the thirties. A Cartier wedding ring with the words "Pax-Amor-Labor" engraved on it. An empty champagne bottle consumed with first lover. An ashtray stolen from a motel in Las Vegas ("very exotic for the French girl"), her grandmother's cartridge pen and an inkwell, three quilts, and a drawing of a horse that first boyfriend drew, never framed.

riage of convenience and comfort has made Americans stand out wherever they roam. Why else, I'm constantly asked, can the French girl spot Americans in France from a mile away? They're the ones who, despite sneakers, baseball cap, overburdened backpack, and all the gear, still look like they're wearing pajamas.

French lounge queen Natalie, who spends her free time carefully picking through Paris's chic vintage boutiques for the ultimate handmade silk mou-mou or the perfectly padded zebra-skin mules, explains it this way: "If you want to feel like you're wearing pajamas, wear them! But do it with style. Buy a pair of men's silk pajama pants from the fifties and wear them with a tight tank. Get eccentric. But be selective. Learn to lounge in style. Why live life in baggy sweat pants and shoes as big as club sandwiches?" While I had nostalgic memories of walking to my local grocer in California wearing little rubber flipflops and (gasp!) sweat pants, Natalie's point is well taken.

The French Signature

For centuries French kings and queens were jewelry junkies. They wore big outrageous crowns, chunky medallions, slinky bracelets, and jeweled earrings. No wonder the French girl instinctively knows how to accessorize.

These days, it's impossible to imagine the French girl—or boy, for that matter—without at least a trademark scarf. (Can you imagine the Little Prince on his desolate little asteroid without his flowing yellow scarf?) Her scarf—twisted, tied, folded, looped, or thrown—adds a finishing touch to anything. It's sophisticated yet bohemian, simple yet luxurious.

Her handbag, for example, is usually small and structured (no giant hobo sacks), tasteful, and holds the bare essentials (a trim wallet, a lipstick, a handkerchief, a cell phone, a good quality pen). She might save for years to buy an Hermès bag, but she'll carry it for the rest of her life.

She wears jewelry with great discretion. Not layers of matching trinkets or heavy pieces that might make good hood ornaments; rather she'll usually wear one fine piece at the neck or the ears or the wrist, perhaps something antique as a focal point. If she wears eyeglasses, they're stylish without being trendy and they act like an accent, not a flaw. In winter, she wears an excellent pair of the softest leather gloves, likely in black.

Le Film

CONTES DES QUATRE SAISONS
(Tales of the Four Seasons)

See Eric Rohmer's four tales for the intelligent dialogue, the natural, believable interaction between skilled but little known actors (there's nary a Depardieu or a Deneuve in sight) and especially for the glimpse at the way French girls dress in day-to-day life. No couture, no clichés, just clothes that probably come right out of the actors' closets.

"An accessory is not just an item you put on your lapel or around your neck," says one French friend. "A real accessory has personal meaning. It's a small extension of oneself." Indeed, the best accessory is distinctive and clearly punctuates the French girl's self-expression.

Fin

It took a few years to shed some of the red, white, and blue biases I had about my own body—and even longer to finally shed my bikini top. But living so long amidst French

"Don't ever wear artistic jewelry; it wrecks a woman's reputation."
COLETTE

girls finally unraveled the seams that had been in the fabric of my American life for so long. The French girl is a reminder that to be truly free, we must reclaim our bodies—and by extension our self-image—from the tyranny (there's no other word!) of certain cultural preconceptions and commercial ideals. We don't have to all look the same. We don't have to aspire to be supermodels. We don't have to *have* more in order to *be* more. The French girl knows that sensuality is her birthright, and to flaunt

How to Tie a Scarf

There are three classic ways the French girl wears a scarf.

Loose: A soft cashmere muffler or woven Italian knit is best for this look. Fold a long scarf in half, end to end. Holding the two ends in one hand and the loop you've made in the other hand, drape the folded scarf around your neck. Pull the two ends through the loop together, tightening as much or as little as you prefer. The ends can either lie down to one side of your body or hang down the center.

Tailored: Make a triangle of a square or rectangular scarf. Place the point down in front of your chest and bring the ends around to the back of your neck. Cross the ends in back and bring them around to the front. Tie a square knot over the triangle and tuck the ends in. The point of the scarf can either be tucked into a blouse or sweater or gently tugged towards one shoulder.

Vieille Dame (old lady): Make a triangle. Drape the pointed end over one shoulder and bring the ends together over the other. Tie a square knot. That's it.

what she's got—rather than endlessly reinvent herself—is the key to enduring feminine power. The French girl unequivocally owns her own life and her own body. And she takes care of both. She strikes her own pose. Rows her own boat. Lives her own life.

Le Livre

MADAME BOVARY
by Gustave Flaubert

Even if you read this in college, read it again right now. The vastness of Emma Bovary's desperate emotions is matched thread for thread, color for color by the aesthetics of her existence—the clothes, the home, the food, the garden. "She mingled in her longing the material pleasures of the senses with the joys of the heart, the refinements of elegant society with the subtle delicacy of feelings." Poor overindulged, unfulfilled Emma.

Writer Erica Jong blew Madame B. this French kiss: "If Emma Bovary, with all her self-delusion, still stirs our hearts, it is because she wants something authentic and important for her life to have meaning, for her life to bring transcendence." Very, very French girl.

Three

Le Coeur

My American friendships often took off from day one in an inspired burst of sisterhood. But the word "sisterhood" does not even exist in the French vocabulary. And so getting to know Marie—entering her inner circle, knowing her intimate secrets—was like crossing uncharted land without a compass. Like a true French girl, Marie gave nothing away at first, not a hint of who she was or how she lived her life. All the bits and pieces of her identity, including the quirky dysfunction that in America we wear on our shirtsleeves, was entirely under lock and cover. We spent our first encounter at her country home. We made an impromptu lunch with simple wine and cheese. There was no small talk between us, but no big talk either. Marie and I were two satellites in a similar orbit (our husbands were working partners, and so our lives were intertwined), and it felt like glacial time before Marie started to reveal herself in ways that would have come fast and furious in America. In fact it took a few years—our children had begun to grow up together, and many bottles of extraordinarily fine wine from their deliciously damp cellar had been consumed over the course of many lengthy meals—before Marie finally leaned over and prefaced her words with, "Please don't repeat what I am about to say . . ." At that moment, we were truly friends. A mysterious combustion had taken place, an invisible but potent mixing of chemistries had created from two distinct entities something you could call sisterhood *à la française*. And it is this slow-brewing process, informed by her sense of history and personal priorities, that underscores almost all of her relationships, and defines the nature of her heart.

Vous/Tu

On many occasions I've watched the French sidestep the direct use of the word "you" to avoid improperly address-ing a person. Such is the delicate and sometimes pains-takingly subtle role of language in French life. So it's no surprise that how the French girl manages every relation-ship lies in the very nature of language itself. From the day she's born, she's learning to manage the delicate bal-ance between the two "yous"—the formal *vous* and the informal *tu*. That involves knowing how to size up a per-son, evaluate their social status, consider proper etiquette given the circumstance at hand, determine what she should and should not say, ponder the invisible bounda-ries that bring people together and keep them apart, and think hard before she speaks—all in about a millisecond. No wonder she's poised. Maintaining distance and pro-tocol (*vous*) or shifting into a familiar, intimate gear (*tu*), the French girl navigates her relationships with a built-in sense of discretion.

In *vous* there is history, sanctity, and propriety. There is both the great and noble sense of order, and neatly de-fined social hierarchy where everyone has his or her place, the clean respectful lines that define where you leave off and the other person picks up. (This goes for first names as well: You're Madame or Monsieur long before you're Betty or Bob.) There is even the nearly sacramental way of ending a letter that persists today:

Who Gets Vous, Who Gets Tu

Back in the old days formal boundaries between individuals were maintained with rigid protocol. These days French society is more hang-loose, though hard rules still do apply:

WHO GETS VOUS
—Your in-laws (probably forever)
—Your boss (though that changes based on industry. In many professions the use of *tu* happens almost instantaneously).
—Certain colleagues and clients (moving from *vous* to *tu* in the workplace is contingent on countless little social cues and nuances).
—Teachers, administrators, bureaucrats and anyone who can wield more red tape than you can.
—The rest of the world: Anyone and everyone you *don't* know who makes up your daily life, from new clients to retailers.
—Your parents: Sometimes, in certain families, where the traces of *la grande bourgeoisie* still linger.

WHO GETS TU
—Friends
—Family members (with the exception of in-laws and *la grande bourgeoisie*)
—Children
—Certain colleagues
—Anyone who merits a certain disdain (the irreverent use of the informal *tu* is an insult in and of itself)

Veuillez agréer, Madame/Monsieur, l'expression de mes sentiments les plus distingués: Please accept, Monsieur/Madame, the expression of my most distinguished sentiments. (Just say "sincerely"? Forget it.)

Despite the loosening up of language the French girl cannot help but respect the boundaries of *vous*: after nearly fifteen years of remonstrations ("Please, let's use *tu*," my husband implores), our nephew's girlfriend still simply cannot possibly address my husband in any way other than the formal *vous*. She knows that while the informal *tu* can get dicey, *vous* will never get you into trouble.

As an American I had *carte blanche* to fumble with language, but while it felt awkward at first trying to figure out who got *vous* or *tu*—and impossibly stuffy hearing someone call me *"Madame"*—I later began to feel a certain comfort in the respectful distance and anonymity in the formal use of language. It created a boundary. A sense of privacy. A little signpost for certain people that said, ever so nicely, "Keep out." I grew so comfortable, in fact, that the first time someone used my first name, after years of calling me simply "Madame," I felt a slight transgression of personal space that made me actually flinch.

The French girl grows up with this precision of language defining, in the most transparent yet concrete fashion, the parameters of her relationships. Is it any wonder that she exudes a sense of self-containment and discretion in the very nature of her relationships to others?

Community Life: The Outer Circle

When I took a visiting American friend to Chartres for the first time, she looked around at its ancient cobblestone streets and its magical *châteaux* and exclaimed, "It looks just like Disneyland!" We Americans have gotten so used to imitation that we confuse it with the real thing—and vice versa. In some respects we've lost a sense of true community life, which is part of what makes France so charming to us. It may be the size of Texas, but France has 36,000 mayors reigning over innumerable regions, districts, and subdistricts, all of which, like Russian dolls, harbor increasingly small and intimate clusters of tightly woven community life. The French girl lives within her own cluster, in a densely packed urban forest, with its culture and commerce, its particular history. She maintains relationships with everyone who services her needs—the butcher, the baker, the candlestick maker—

"You call me *vous*. *Vous* yourself! . . . Ah! Wretch, how could you have written this letter? How cold it is? . . . Hell has no torments great enough! Nor do the Furies have serpents enough! *Vous! Vous!*"
NAPOLEON BONAPARTE, IN
CORRESPONDENCE WITH JOSEPHINE.

and the enduring regularity of these relationships are the very bedrock of her daily life.

These relationships are the outer ring of her inner circle, and without them her life would be bereft of the professional counsel that puts the art in real living. And so, in ways that would make a busy, convenience-oriented American wince, she has an investment in them all: The baker who makes sure that a steamy fresh loaf of *pain aux noix et le comté* is put aside for her before the Sunday rush. The postman who delivers her mail come rain, shine, or interminable postal strike. The farmers at her local open market who guide her to the freshest produce, tell her what to bake (and how) with her *blanquette de veau aux pistaches*, and run a tab if she's short on cash. The proprietor of her local boutique, who invites her to a private preview of the season's offerings. Or the patron of the chocolate shop, who offers her a delectable piece of dark chocolate to brighten up a rainy morning.

Like the clear lines drawn by the use of *vous*, these relationships require a certain distinction and formality. Violate them at your own risk. Early one morning in Paris, I stumbled upon a café owner raising the noisy metal shutters to her establishment. Rushed and in desperate need of an espresso, I briskly asked this patroness of my Parisian *petit déjeuner* what time her café opened. She turned quietly with key still in hand and, with a half-smile, said firmly: "First we say 'Excuse me, Madame. Hello and good morning.' And *then* we ask what time the café opens." I stood corrected. Curiously, the French girl may be an iconoclast at heart, but she still has a fastidious attachment to certain tenacious little formalities.

The French Girl Is an Exclusive Club of One

I'd known one of my closest French girlfriends nearly ten years before I learned that she came from a noble family, with a string of majestically dilapidated *châteaux* scattered around the hexagon and an uncle who was anointed a sovereign saint. Likewise, I'd known another girlfriend for many years (we spent summers together, our sons were like brothers) before she revealed some slightly salacious and intriguing details about her life that would have been headline news in any other American friendship from the get-go. True to form, it took time to become part of their inner circle: The door opened a tiny crack at first, with barely a glimpse of the stage on which their private lives unfolded. Like typical French girls, they considered the American girl's general affability (her desire

Le Film

ENTRE NOUS

This film, set in the 50s, rings with a certain emotional truth about the nature of female friendship, *à la française*. Madeleine (played by Miou-Miou) and Lena (Isabelle Huppert) meet by chance and develop a rich, intense bond, against the backdrop of their relationships with their respective families. See it for the insight about French-girl friendship during the postwar years. And see it because of Miou-Miou and Huppert, two French girls extraordinaires.

to gather a wide group of acquaintances, to quickly become best friends, and to easily say "I love you") as a sign of superficiality. The American girl, of course, considers the French girl's restraint and singular focus on an exclusive group of friends—and her love of solitude, even in public—as a slightly close-minded *hauteur*. The reality lies somewhere between the two.

The French girl does indeed move in a closed ecosystem of her own. She chooses her friends with the same ongoing discretion that informs all of her other choices in life. She won't easily reveal her family secrets. Or her conjugal woes. She won't even tell you where she got her new Céline dress (it was on sale, but that's her little secret). She won't divulge much or open her heart too wide until she feels the relationship is authentic, about trust, and grounded in quality.

> ## *Borrow A Page From the French Girl's Book: Friendship*
>
> Cultivate friendships instead of collecting them. Deepen and clarify existing relationships before adding new ones. Go slowly in getting to know someone, allowing the friendship to unfold rather than burst into bloom. Share your secrets sparingly; guard the secrets others share with you. Invite friends into your home thoughtfully and as a meaningful gesture of friendship. Nurture and protect the lives around you.

One of the first signs that the guard rail has lifted is when the French girl invites you to her home for a meal. Inviting you *chez elle* means that she is quite literally opening the doors of her personal life. (The French are often both bewildered and charmed by the open-door, open-house policies of Americans.) And once you've crossed that threshold, a new frontier in friendship emerges.

Family

In France the word "dysfunction" usually refers to your broken VCR. In America, it invariably refers to your family. Enough said? One of the most useful and frequently employed terms in the French vocabulary is "*point de repère*." It signifies both a concrete, physical signpost (a

What She Shares, What She Keeps To Herself

WHAT SHE SHARES (BUT NOT IN UNDUE DETAIL):

What she's reading, her favorite films, recipes, work ennui (though that's low on the totem pole), political opinions (though if she senses you're not in her camp, she'll be discreet), vacation plans, school issues, anything related to community life at large.

WHAT SHE KEEPS TO HERSELF (UNTIL SHE KNOWS YOU WELL):

Family secrets, marriage secrets (does her husband have a mistress? Is *she* a mistress?), anything related to money (what she makes for a living, how much her car cost, etc.), her dress size, what she thinks of your family, her doubts or insecurities, her long-term dreams and aspirations.

landmark, say) and an emotional milestone or point of reference. In France the family is the French girl's primary and essential *point de repère*. It anchors her against the seas of change through enduring traditions, and prevents her from having any interest in that particularly American brand of soul searching that sends one adrift into the busy wilderness of self-help.

In even the most fragmented French families, the French girl accepts character flaws as the inevitable part of human nature; history has taught her to accept the inevitable strangeness of human foibles, particularly in family life. "They're all nuts but I'm not a victim of their craziness," says Frédérique of her large, eccentric family. "Without them I'd still be only half a person."

There is something about the zealous quest for personal transformation that sends shivers up the French girl's spine. It's not that she doesn't love her shrink; it's that like cooking or cultivating a look, her sense of self-improvement—which in and of itself is an utterly American concept—comes from a long, slow-brewing wrestling with basic human elements. It's a lifetime project, a subtle steady undercurrent that feels old, not new.

Therapists aside, the French girl is far more likely to cull wisdom from the pages of Michel Foucault or the advice of a savvy older aunt than she is from a post-modern mystic or family therapy. When it comes to self-help, she is stubbornly fatalistic. "I'm not sure which is more lunatic," says Frédérique, "trying to change yourself constantly, or trying to change other people."

"It is wise to apply the oil of refined politeness to the mechanism of friendship."
COLETTE

A Dog's Life

One afternoon on the Champs Elysées, I noticed a French girl crossing the street with a dog in her arms and a child on a kiddie leash. It was an aberration, but it pretty much summed up the elevated status of the dog in French life. "Toutou" is a real *chéri*, and he is everywhere. He's allowed in restaurants and on public beaches. In hotels and at business meetings. He's a bona fide citizen of the French republic and, in some ways, he's the wild side of the Cartesian self; the little furry Jerry Lewis of the French soul. His natural indiscretions are tolerated for this very reason (several tons of indiscretions, to be precise, which are cleaned up daily from French streets), and he is the exception to the enduring role that time plays in cultivating relationships in France. When you have a dog in France, you're immediately part of an intimate fraternity, a closed sub-culture of canine lovers. The French dog is imperial and the best way to walk directly into the heart of the French girl is to do so, quite literally, on the tail of her dog.

Family History

Scratch the surface of a traditional American family and you'll find the edge of a continent and faded memories. Scratch the surface of a traditional French family and you'll find buried treasures, scary secrets, wars, feasts, and famines. While a ruined *château* or a coat of arms might be part of the French girl's legacy, most French families have a profound and ancestral connection to the land—tilling it, harvesting it, and living by the seasonal shifts of weather.

Many of these families still live on the same plots of land, in the same towns, as they have for generations, and express astonishment at the American drive to keep working until one is well past one's prime. After a lifetime of service filling the nation's coffers with taxes, the French settle into their country homes, their gardens, their apartments; they fill the decks of cruise ships or simply enjoy the pleasures of city life. They're out there shopping, reading the paper, poking at the skins of early tomatoes in markets or negotiating the price of house wine. In some parts of France, where the slow rural pace of country life has sent French youth clamoring for big cities, they are omnipresent. (Clearly, the privilege of working a lifetime is the freedom not to work at all.)

And their memories live on. Contrary to the customs in my hometown of Los Angeles, where people don't seem to age but simply vanish beyond well-manicured lawns, generations of my adopted French family have come to rest like other French families, in a well-tended village cemetery where elaborate tombstones and ornate funerary objects pay homage to those who came before. Their ghosts live on in vestiges of their past—their homes, their antiques, their gardens still blooming with heirloom vegetables and extravagant fruit trees tended by extended family and friends.

The French Family Tree

The French family tree usually contains an eclectic and rangy mix of immediate and extended members who remain characters in each other's lives for the duration. There's nothing neat and tidy about them, but they represent a familiar jumble of history and habit and quirks and affection that defines the French family.

Take my friend, Laurent. His family is a cast of uptight bankers, lawyers, various civil servants, and bureaucrats who were, a few generations back, part of reigning nobility. His family is big and *bourgeois*, and Laurent takes great pains to avoid them as much as possible. They have a *château* near Lyon, but like many it's gone to pot because the family can't afford to maintain it (these hulking spaces have bad roofs, ancient plumbing, erratic electricity, and more—magnificent but untenable). Laurent is burdened by his family's "smallness of spirit and Proustian pretensions" but has learned to accept them all with almost courtly politesse. The big *bourgeois* family that people love to hate is not unusual in France.

The professors and intellectuals in Sophie's family spend their lives among books and are more or less subsidized by the government to sit around and think. She also has a handful of shrinks in her family, inspired by the likes of Freud and Foucault, and a few tormented souls who ended their days in dramatic depressions and

histrionic family dramas. "The stuff of French novels,"
says Sophie. "Part Balzac, part pulp fiction. That's my
family."

Some can trace their family back to the Huguenots.
Some come from distant colonies. Some have a nun in the
family, or a landowner who once rented a swatch of farm-
land to local peasants for tilling and harvesting. Of course
there are also the cheesemakers, winemakers, vineyard
owners, and farmers.

Mothers

Before she finally became a mother, seven long years after
she married Louis XVI, Marie Antoinette lamented, "If
only I were a mother, I should be considered a French
woman."

The French mother is often the source of everything that informs the French girl: a sense of the feminine, of social conduct, poise, etiquette and, of course, cooking. She's an arbiter of continuity and tradition, a sort of magistrate who oversees the smooth functioning of family life—managing conflict, diffusing resentments, letting go of grudges in an elegant and seemingly transparent way. Through her all things eventually pass—the family's history as living memory as well as the future—and in many cases the younger French girl (and French boy, for that matter) will live *chez Maman* well into their twenties.

And then there is the French grandmother.

I met Chloé's grandmother one blustery afternoon in the courtyard of our apartment complex. She was sitting on a bench dressed in her finest (heels, pearls, silk scarf, elegant hairpin in a thick grey chignon, impeccable ruby lips), watching over Chloé's two well-behaved children, who wore bright galoshes and were scrambling for a pail and shovel from my decidedly less well-behaved son. Chloé's grandmother—Madame Perrin, I would later learn—nodded respectfully as I sat down beside her. "You

"The French woman rules French life, and she rules it under a triple crown, as a business woman, as a mother, and above all, as an artist."
EDITH WHARTON

must be the American," she said, as if I'd been sporting the stars and stripes. (In fact, Madame Perrin had spotted me speaking English to my son at the baker's weeks earlier and had, through that very discreet but no less effective French grapevine, found out some salient details about my life.)

Madame Perrin and I would become regulars on that little bench. She was omnipresent in her grandchildren's lives—picking them up from school, making dinner when Chloé came home late, taking them to pediatric appointments and carting them off with her to their country home on Easter and summer breaks. She would storm through the sand in her heels (perfectly poised, somehow) if they misbehaved, bake them elaborate cakes on holidays, and correct them if they spoke out of line. She had a sweet voice and a stern presence and would use them both to underscore her grandparenting authority with even—yes, sometimes—a little remonstrative spanking on the side.

I met many variations on Madame Perrin over the years: The typical French grandmother is not living in the equivalent of a French Florida or, conversely, still working full-time at her career. She's the recipient of a relatively generous retirement pension from the French government and is bequeathed the luxury of time. Like Madame Perrin she still lives close to her children or in the family's country home—often an enchanted house with a mythic sense of place that's been passed down for generations, and to which the family returns on a regular

What The French Girl Inherits from Her Mother

An old pair of Chanel sunglasses. Great hair. Limoges dishes. Lots of pride and a Roman nose. An Hermès scarf from the fifties. Diamond earrings. The ability to bake anything from scratch. A gold cigarette case. Love letters from a long-lost GI. A sense of irony. A collection of cigar boxes. What it takes to be poor and still live in style.

basis. Urban or provincial, the French grandmother is often still an integral part of family life, a sort of reigning queen whose accrued wisdom keeps the family knitted together in a greater historical context.

My own mother—my busy, working, New World, American mom—passed on certain values to me. The value of risk taking. Of empathy. Of questioning authority. My French mother-in-law, on the other hand, passed on linens.

The linens are from the turn of the century (that's the twentieth century). Long and furrowed, with ancient embossed edges, the linens are so roughly hewn you can almost feel the pulpy heaviness of the original cotton fibers. These days who could possibly appreciate (let alone use) these venerable old linens when people are slipping into 360-count sateen cotton sheets as smooth as silk?

My French mother-in-law ran an inn in the Loire Valley, and for decades these linens brought comfort to pre-and post-war wanderers. They were washed in boilers, fluffed and folded. They were tucked neatly under stately old beds and pulled back from large rumpled down pillows. But for years they've been unused and stacked up in great, folded, cream-colored heaps in an old, splintered pine armoire. They take up space where other, more useful items might be stored. Still, I can't get rid of them. They're a piece of the past, they're a reminder of the sheer pleasure of authentic, more rugged comforts our modern luxuries have irrevocably replaced.

One day I might take them out and actually use them. Or, more likely, I'll pass them onto my own daughter. The American part of her might donate them to charity or chuck them altogether. But with a little luck, the French part of her, with its appreciation for the authentic and the frayed edges of history, will keep them.

Le Livre

LE DIVORCE
by Diane Johnson

Johnson's contemporary novel *Le Divorce*, offers a somewhat upper-crusty view of Parisians who all "come with three pieces of real-estate." Still, *Le Divorce* pokes good fun at the French and Americans and touches on love, lust, marriage, and, of course, divorce.

> ## Borrow A Page From the French Girl's Book: Family
>
> Consider your family as an essential continuum, even if it's small or fragmented. Perpetuate your family's collective memory and personal history by preserving and passing down meaningful objects. Establish a couple of rituals (a big dinner once a week, a family brunch, a walk *en famille* after Thanksgiving dinner) and maintain them at all costs. Keep photo albums and scrap books; jot down captions in good ink.

Children and Family

When I returned to the States for the first time after giving birth in France, I was astonished: A vast kingdom of baby merchandise was at my disposal as a new mother, entire stores dedicated to breast pumps, musical potties, modular high chairs, high-performance bibs and child-security devices for every conceivable wall, door, drawer, toilet, ledge, and edge.

Here the child was both a liability and a marvel, a commodity and an inspired creature. In France I had cruised the aisles of supermarkets and ventured into the no man's land of the suburban Île-de-France looking in vain for what was copiously, extravagantly on sale everywhere in America. I ecstatically stocked up on everything (later, French mothers, pushing three kids in the same recycled stroller and making do with basic cutlery and simple toys, would look quizzically at my postmodern nursing bras and my super-stylized sippy cups); only later did the flipside of this material abundance dawn on me: That it was, in some respects, a noisy replacement for something more fundamental that had been lost in the boomer years, something more age-old and practical and simple: essentially, how in the world to truly parent.

Maybe that's why despite globalization (little Johnny and little Jean might both have the same Gap cap or pair of Skechers), there is still something that distinguishes American children from their French counterparts: Where the American child bears the stamp of a certain tempestuous air of privilege and plenty—and the mark of a particular strain of ambivalent permissiveness—the French child is simply the most recent in a long line of progeniture. He/she is hemmed in by tradition, by an almost folkloric common sense and conventional wisdom. There is less freedom in this context but also a greater sense of history and responsibility. There is also a clearer notion of boundaries and, if nothing else, the uncanny ability to do much more meaningful parenting with far less stuff.

Not long ago French children were considered little adults: miniature big people who came into the world to take on their parents' trade, to till the land, churn the butter, carry on the family business. Their images are preserved in sienna photographs and daguerreotypes, serious little faces looking out from the mists of time.

French Girls We Love
MARIE ANTOINETTE

For still fascinating us, more than two hundred years later. She was petulant, frivolous, and immature. She was an avid gambler and a willing slave to her many other vices and amusements. She had almost total contempt for public opinion, but she was also utterly charming, a loving and devoted mother, and the foremother of women's lib—who do you think loosed us from the corset, for slipper's sake? Read Antonia Fraser's *Marie Antoinette: The Journey*.

Today French children are much more like kids, though compared to her American counterpart the French girl still grows up with the expectation that she will behave like a small grown-up. Before she dons her first pair of high heels or opens her first lipstick, the French girl knows this: Expectations are upheld not only by her family, but by the culture at large.

In France, children don't run the show, adults do. And parenting is one of the rare instances where the French are actually more direct than Americans. Instead of "Please cooperate with your mother or you will get a consequence," the French come right out with it: "Obey your mother or you'll be punished." That might be followed by a little slap on the rump, which won't raise any eyebrows unless those eyebrows belong to American tourists.

French children are also rarely accorded certain adult

luxuries. War, scarcity, socialist underpinnings, and an appreciation for authenticity have taught the French that frugality is a virtue, and that its value must be taught at an early age. So little Pierre may get only one toy not ten, no matter how much he protests. (Furthermore, his toys will stay in his room. The toy-strewn, child-trodden living rooms that you see in the States just don't happen in France.) With a structured, adult-centered family life the French girl grows up understanding boundaries of all sorts and respecting them. She grows up, once again, like a grown-up: She is brought up eating lavishly and regularly at the table, sitting correctly, not watching TV while she eats but finishing her courses. She will grow up observing the etiquette of language (*"Oui, Monsieur/Madame," "Merci beaucoup, Monsieur/Madame"*), respecting her elders, fearing authority (later, she'll learn to question it, then ignore it), and accepting the constraints of a culture that does not always welcome her (take restaurants, for starters). Where the American will grasp their children's hands for dear life at a crosswalk, the French child learns to stand on his/her own at an intersection (particularly disturbing to witness at Parisian rush hour) or plays in what would be considered, by American standards, high-risk environments. Where toddlers abound I've seen steep staircases with no banisters or child gates, public jungle gyms with hair-raising drops onto unforgiving concrete, unsupervised kiddie pools that approached mayhem. "So your kid falls down and bumps his head," one French mother offered when I expressed concern over a perilous-looking set of swings with no safety belts. "How else is he going to learn how to swing?" The French girl might grow up in a world of clear social conduct, but she also learns in a school of hard knocks.

In considering the ways of the French girl, it's impossible not to consider how children fit into French life on an even grander scale. As a society it's easy to pay lip service to family values, much harder to promote the value of the family. It's in the latter case that the French excel, attending to the welfare of their children like little crops: socialized medicine for all, including free maternity and post-natal care (if a child is too sick to go to the doctor, the doctor will go to the child). There's affordable daycare for all, free high-quality nursery schools, a system of certified, state-subsidized nannies, and cash allocations for every child added to a family. Who could ask for more?

Who Teaches Children What

As a child the French girl grows up in a large adult community of de facto advisors or etiquette coachs. There's the neighbor who feels free (and *is* free) to admonish another neighbor's child ("You must *never* shake hands with your left hand." "You must *always* wear your hat over your ears in cold weather." "If you throw that ball against the brick wall one more time you will be punished!") or the school administrator who, far from being the American-style, sympathetic, garden-variety diplomat with an open-door policy, is more likely a critical disciplinarian who is more concerned about teaching Paulette to respect authority than to nurture her self-esteem (and who will discuss that very subject with you strictly by appointment only from behind the large locked doors of the school's two-ton nineteenth-century portal).

If something unpleasant happens (say, Jean-Claude kicks Pierre in the mouth and knocks out a tooth), everyone is in a position to set the child right with a healthy dose of criticism. (The fact that no one is likely to get sued makes it all the more easy for parents to jump into the fray.)

Children and Time

The French child's life is divided into two distinct halves: There's school life. And there's family life. In between, the pickings aren't necessarily slim, but they're not the same American smorgasbord of unlimited, nonstop activities, either. The French child is not busy to the point of being stressed and overbooked because the French are naturally inclined to resist the impulse to fill every moment with things that vie for a child's attention.

The French child experiences life revolving like a great European chronometer not by the calendar year, but by the beginning of the new school year. Called "*la rentrée*" (literally, "the return"), this is when the tide rolls back after a long, languorous summer and the next cycle of working life rises to an imposing height. The streets are literally filled with French children towing colossal

Brief Words of Parenting Wisdom from a French Mother.

On time: "I believe that boredom is one of the most formative experiences in childhood. Kids must learn to be creative on their own instead of constantly being entertained and distracted. They must take the time to be children. They must learn the fine art of doing nothing in particular."

On things: "Children's lives are saturated with objects. It's overwhelming. I've started something radical: Only one birthday present per year. People think I'm crazy but I can assure you my children have learned to appreciate things in life this way. They've also learned to be ingenious the old-fashioned way: with twigs, pots and pans, a few paints, and their imagination."

On meals: "What's there to say? They must always be eaten *en famille*. Is there any other way?"

On child-rearing in general: "To be a good parent you must practice patience, pleasure, empathy, and gentle authority. You must also learn to let go. It may often feel like our children own us, but we certainly do not own them."

schoolbags stocked with hardback texts and graph-ruled notebooks. Unlike American "back to school" rhythms, *la rentrée* heralds the start of a new series of holidays and three-day weekends, giving parents more time with their kids, not less.

Borrow A Page From the French Girl's Book: Children

Embrace boundaries and structure in family life. Be a parent first, then a friend. Surround your child with authentic things and experiences. Expose your child to the real world. Work with local charities. Volunteer at a soup kitchen. Resist the desire to fill every moment with activities. Take the time to be with your child and teach him/her the virtues of time and solitude. Encourage daydreaming, reverie, and thoughtfulness in your children. Teach them the value of delayed gratification.

Men and Women

Before children—before marriage and babies—there's the dating scene, and the art of seduction, in its countless subtle expressions (and it's almost always subtle, even as it boldly advances). Veteran dater Analise describes the French dating scene this way: "Either you're having a little 'adventure' (read: one-night stand), in which case things happen spontaneously and freely. Or, if there's really interest on the part of two people, things take time. Lots of time. Seduction is a big part of the dating dynamic in France: We're subtle, not direct. Men still have to woo the old-fashioned way, with flowers, homemade dinners, good wine, that sort of thing. Women need to keep their interest to themselves, yes, maybe play a little hard to get in a nice way. And everyone—men and women—want to be seduced by the mind. If you're good looking, that helps. But if you're good looking with nothing upstairs, you're out of luck. So if you want to date successfully, you've got to have intellectual curiosity, wit, a well-read mind, and a sense of irony."

One of the eminently practical attributes of the French girl's sense of self-possession and her rejection of the quick fix is her way with men. Where they don't find fulfillment in a man, Cécile argues, they find it elsewhere. "If a shoe doesn't fit, you don't buy it. Your foot isn't going to change its shape, right? Same goes for men. If he's not right for you, drop him. Unless you want to walk around in pain, you move on to new merchandise. It's really that simple, no?"

Further, the French girl knows inherently that the point is never to change the man. Says Cécile: "We know that human nature is what it is. We're all a bunch of romantic cynics."

Even when she's in the middle of love's slings and arrows, the French girl has a certain *sang froid* about her. She doesn't stray far from her own emotional center, and tends to her own needs even in the midst of personal drama.

Underpinning this state of mind is the relative freedom she feels as a single girl. Where the American media preys on the American girl with mixed messages about her bi-

Le Film

JULES ET JIM

See this classic, which is one of Truffaut's masterpieces, for the way it turns the classic French triangle formula of a man with two women into a New Wave triangle comprised of a woman with two men. Played by the young Jeanne Moreau, she exerts a magnetic life force that attracts best friends, Jules and Jim. Eventually, the radiant, sensual Catherine marries Jules, but the threesome continue to come together in a variety of combinations that explore every facet of love and friendship between men and women—French style.

ological clock (all the hand-wringing and hair-pulling over marriage and baby making; all the talk of spiritual death for women who are bereft of both past the age of forty), the French girl is not stigmatized with the same pressures. Yes, there are French dating services and online romances and women who long desperately for mates, but the ferocious anguish that is publicly trumpeted for the dubious benefit of the single American girl is far less apparent.

And if the French girl's private longings become larger than life, she'll take action the old fashioned way. "The French girl can't walk into a sperm bank or meet an egg donor and have a child. That is very heavily legislated in France; it is not big business," says Cécile. "But why a sperm bank, anyhow? There's plenty of sperm to be had. If a French girl wants a baby, she does it the way women have done it for centuries. Sex without love, purely for reproductive purposes, can be found everywhere. And the independent woman who wants a child is free to do this, without the government's permission, without paying a fortune, and without it being anyone's business but her own."

The French girl plays the dating game her own way (and she's well aware that it's a game). It's back to that powerful sense of self-possession that tempers all things, including the slippery slopes of love. When Don Juan or Monsieur Right comes knocking on her door, she never throws her heart wide open. Her cards are held close to the vest. The art of seduction unfurls in a dance of coded restraint. Is this what makes a classic coquette? Maybe. But despite her reputation as a love goddess, she's about subtle sensuality, not in-your-face sexuality. Flirting, which is a fine art in France, is part of the dance and does not offend the feminist in the French girl. A friend explains, "French feminism has few of the sharp edges it has in America. In France, it's softer, fuzzier. The French girl can be a feminist and still unequivocally love men."

Ultimately, the French girl seduces by revealing very little about herself. She never swings her private door wide open—*Howdy! Come on in!*—and is not necessarily quick to hop in the sack. (French teenagers are much less inclined to engage in recreational sex than their American counterparts.) She has no preconceived notion of the per-

French Girls We Love

ANAÏS NIN

For choosing her own path as a woman, writer, wife, and lover. A sexual libertine, prolific diarist, and feminist icon, Nin pretty much did what she wanted to do. And everything she did she wrote about. Extremely attractive to men throughout her long life, Nin enjoyed many single sexual encounters, affairs, and even a stable if unconventional marriage—remarkably, all at once! She wrote literary erotica, novels, poetry, and, of course, her famously controversial diaries. See the film *Henry and June*. Read *A Literary Passion*, which includes many letters exchanged between Nin and longtime lover Henry Miller. Also read Dierdre Blair's *Anaïs Nin*, and Nin's own posthumously published collection of erotic stories, *The Delta of Venus*.

---

fect man or the perfect couple. And she doesn't need everything set in stone or checked off a list.

The French date varies: It might be an intellectual sortie to hear a lecture or an opera; it might be a simple evening at the movies or dinner at a favorite local haunt. What sets a different tenor to the scene has more to do with the quiet language that brings two people into closer emotional proximity—the unspoken as well as the spoken, the implicit as well as the explicit.

"I've dated French women for months before I ever really knew who they were," says Christophe. "After the first or second date, the American woman wants everything spelled out: 'Are we dating? Are you my boyfriend or just a friend? Now that we've made love, are we a couple?' There's a big emphasis on defining things up front. A French woman does not do that. She doesn't give much away. She's comfortable letting things evolve naturally, but the ball's almost always in her court."

Saying I Do

The French girl says "I don't" long before she says "I do." Cohabitation is the trend throughout Europe, and while everyone loves the pomp and circumstance of marriage, cohabitation is so prevalent that the government has passed legislation protecting unmarried partners and their children. "We had two kids before we married," says Geneviève. "When we finally married, it was for practical reasons: to get a tax break. Emotionally, we've been solidly married for years."

When wedding bells *do* toll for the French girl they often toll quietly and in private, with a small inner circle of family and friends gathered under the cloisters of a local

"The French attach a great deal of importance to love-making, but they consider it more simply and less solemnly than we."
EDITH WHARTON

church. Unless she's a movie star or the prime minister's daughter, you won't see her wedding announced in the local paper, and certainly no prenuptial photos of her and her fiancé smiling back at indifferent readers. Part of this is suspicion, part of it is knowledge that human relationships sometimes do not withstand the unknown tempests of change. Either way, an intractable sense of privacy and discretion are once again the reigning principles here. She might still throw a colossal party with all the trimmings, but the ceremony itself and everything that precedes her wedding is a private affair.

Anatomy of a French Marriage

The French girl is a combination of mistress, madame, and European den mother, and the anatomy of her married life is a little like an x-ray: At first glance it appears like any other complex latticework of sturdy yet delicate bonds. But upon closer inspection you'll notice a certain easing of the joints here, a little flexibility there. The French are Latin souls and have been living and loving long enough to accept with a certain unflinching good humor basic human needs, woes, and contradictions. And on the long, complicated menu of human passions that might be dished out in this regard, the *plat de résistance* would have to be the extra-marital affair.

Not everyone has—or is—a mistress, though the mistress has her place in French culture, and history is flush with tales of her pyrotechnics. Former President of the

French Girls We Love
MADAME DE POMPADOUR

For being elaborately over the top in her ardent affinities for art, architecture and literature, so much so as to have given definition (and her name) to the style of her times. Voltaire has Madame de Pompadour to thank for enabling his career, as do scores of painters, sculptors, and other artists and craftsmen who benefited from her patronage and passions. Sure, she led Louis XIV around by the nose. And she was inordinately preoccupied with elite excesses. But she was a French girl who was very aware of her power and knew exactly where she wanted to go—and learned everything she needed to, from upper-class locution to highbrow philoso phy, to get there. Read Nancy Mitford's *Madame de Pompadour* or *Madame de Pompadour: Images of a Mistress* by Colin Jones.

Republic, François Mitterand, is only the most recent and most high-profile example of the enduring and accepted role of *liaisons dangereuses* in French life. During Mitterand's funeral ceremony his wife, his mistress, and assorted children stood side by side. No one batted an eye. But the affair is certainly not the exclusive domain of the elite.

Take Vivienne, a self-possessed woman of forty-plus years, who's been married to a prominent executive for nearly twenty years. Vivienne's husband has had a mistress for nearly half of their marriage. Vivienne herself, she confides one evening over a glass of Veuve Clicquot, has had her own lover—though her tryst was short lived. (I had known Vivienne for eight years before she confided in me.) Rather than view her husband's "other life" as an indecent transgression of their marital vows, she sees it as a perfectly natural coupling that doesn't threaten her marriage but actually makes it more livable. When pressed on the details, she offered this matter-of-fact commentary: "Listen, men have their needs. So do women. It is very unusual for the sex life of a couple to remain at peak levels for nearly two decades. My husband and I are faithful to one another as spouses, as loving friends. But his private needs are, well, private. So are mine. Better to have him satisfy himself with one mistress over the years than become a serial womanizer, which of course would be perfectly unacceptable."

Not every French girl shares Vivienne's sentiments—and jealousy knows no cultural boundaries—but there is a certain Latin acceptance of the inherent passion in the emotional world *chez la femme française*. Corinne puts it this way: "We're French, so we love to love. But we're also

"I've seen the way you behave with women. In that respect, you are totally unreliable, but we could have an interesting life together."

PAULINE DE ROTHSCHILD, IN HER PROPOSAL
TO HER HUSBAND, BARON PHILIPPE
DE ROTHSCHILD

Le Livre

PASSION SIMPLE
by Annie Ernaux

In expressive yet spare prose, Ernaux limns the landscape of her childhood, her parents, her love affairs. As one *New York Times* reviewer wrote, "With words, she lays open a life—not only her own but others' as well—mother, father, lover, friend. Keen language and unwavering focus allow her to penetrate deep, to reveal pulses of love, desire, remorse." *Passion Simple*, published in 1998, paints a vivid picture of a woman's affair with a married man. Exquisite details such as the clothes she chooses to please him, the fruit and various delicacies she buys for their rendezvous, the art she sees everywhere reminding her of him—all combine to reveal the point of passion.

Cartesian, so we can put things in an intellectual perspective and detach. A little detachment goes a long way in marriage."

A little detachment goes a long way not just in the French girl's marriage. Her self-containment and her natural discretion converge to create a particular brand of impartiality, a sort of a neutrality that doesn't assume things without the proper investment of time and intimacy. That goes for everything: friends, material things, where she spends her time. And where the American girl is more likely to throw herself headlong into new things, the French girl will step back, exercise restraint, keep an intellectual distance before wholeheartedly embracing anything—though it's precisely the American girl's liberal and sometimes tempestuous acceptance of new things that the French girl secretly admires.

Edith Wharton, with her long historical view and her delicate treatment of the emotions, perhaps best sums up the French view of that "disturbing element" called love in marriage when she writes, "[Love] moves to a different rhythm, and keeps different seasons . . . in the relations between grown people, apart from their permanent ties (and in the deepest consciousness of the French, marriage still remains indissoluble), they allow it, frankly and amply."

"If," Wharton continues, "being 'grown up' consists in having a larger and more liberal experience of life, in being less concerned with trifles, less afraid of strong feelings, passions and risks, then the French woman is distinctly more grown up than her American sister."

Le Film

LE BONHEUR

The title of Agnès Varda's gorgeous movie *Le Bonheur* translates as "happiness." The Drouot family is idyllically happy, from the stable, carpenter husband to the beautiful, loving wife to their two lovely children. But this is France, and so the husband decides to add to the family's contentment by adding a mistress to their domestic life. Instead of unraveling the fabric of happiness, this addition re-weaves its texture into a new version of joys of the heart.

The French Kiss

I was with my husband on a film shoot in southern France the first time I had to do the traditional French "*bise*." The crew, thirty strong, was sitting around a series of long tables, aggressively smoking, eating, and laughing. My husband introduced me to a technician at one end of the table, and thus began a long, complicated maneuvering around the tightly packed tables to kiss each crew member on the cheek, twice. The process took approximately ten minutes and involved interrupting numerous conversations and avoiding the luminous butts of many cigarettes, but such was the nature of saying hello. As an American girl fresh off the boat, I would have liked to simply wave across the table, but when in Rome, you know?

For the French girl, of course, *faire la bise* is as basic as (what appears to her to be) the somewhat impersonal handshake or the polite wave from afar. It's a sweet contradiction that in a culture where the conventions of language keep people at a respectful distance (that *vous/tu* thing again), a little intimate pecking on the cheek is the only way to say hello. Then again, we're talking about the French, and what could be more French than a sweet contradiction?

The Language of Love

In the wistful fields of youth lies a tiny metaphor on the language of love: As young American girls we sit in our fields of daisies, pulling off petals with "He loves me, he loves me not." Meanwhile, the little French girl sits in *her* meadow with her *marguerites* and pulls off petals with "He loves me a little. A lot. Passionately. Madly. Not at all." Why does the little French girl innately think in nuances and increasing levels of passion, while we're mired in the black and white of total love and utter rejection? And how can one word—*aimer* in French—mean both to like and to love, when in between the two feelings lies a whole world of emotional intensity?

Part of it may have to do with the fact that we Americans love to be loved. We use the word at almost any occasion ("Love you!" we say in parting to our hair stylist as well as to our closet friend on earth). We swing between two extremes in a frenetic pursuit of love, while the French girl is gracefully hitting balls back and forth in a game of flirtation and seduction, for the sheer, sensual joy of it. She's open to the nuances of life, to the ambiguity of emotion.

When it comes to love, the French are far more interested in gender differences than in gender equality. Maybe that's why the French find it hard to "just be friends" with members of the opposite sex. "There is always sexual tension going on," says Claudine, "or at least sexual curiosity, even if you're just talking to the postman. To deny that is to deny basic human nature." When the French say *vive la différence*, they really mean it.

Borrow A Page From the French Girl's Book: Men

Let go of the myth of the perfect man. (It's a myth, after all.) Focus on your power as an individual and on cultivating authentic relationships. If a relationship isn't working, move on. If you think you can fix your man, think again. Maintain your inner strength. Practice poise by what you don't give away about yourself. Cultivate the life of your mind. Never apologize for who you truly are.

Fin

When it comes to the world of relationships, I love the French girl and I love the American girl. Despite the obvious contradictions, I love the French girl's infallible sense of discretion and respect for boundaries. I love the way she cultivates relationships with such passion and singular focus—including her relationship to herself. And I love the way she keeps her secrets—there are no beans to spill here, no heart aching on her shirtsleeve. That said, I love the American girl precisely, in some instances, for that heart on that shirtsleeve—or for having enough lightness of being to open up easily, without hesitation. I love the American girl for her affability and even, sometimes, for her good-hearted naiveté. And I love the way she'll let her hair down and cultivate, without even trying, that

American thing called sisterhood. If you could fuse them together, you'd get someone who could walk circles around men, keep innumerable secrets, hold her head high come what may, live her own life with passion and flair, and remain mindful of the emotional land that others live in.

Four

La Cuisine

It was one of the worst storms in a decade. It swept through France, toppled telephone poles, flipped cars, and razed forests before it thrashed its way across Spain and on to the Mediterranean. But the storm didn't stop the dinner party. It didn't stop Annie, my husband's *bon vivant* sister, from cooking a lavish five-course meal in her tiny cupboard-lined kitchen, with her big dog Ulysses crouched under a table half his size. It didn't stop the company—a group of travel-weary Frenchmen with their assorted wives and love interests—from driving down France's national highway and then along the crooked roads that wound through beet fields to get to Annie's stone country house, with its big floor-to-ceiling windows and its man-sized fireplace. And it didn't stop the party at large when the electricity went out and the candles went on—big cones of real beeswax and blue votives in small glass jars.

The dinner party took place around a long, wooden table that was simply dressed with a clean white linen tablecloth and small bouquets of wildflowers at each end. The meal was preceded by champagne, homemade *foie gras* and *petits fours*. Cigarette smoke began to do what it always does in France, billowing around the room in a great cloud of silver haze. The dinner was eaten over the span of five leisurely hours, and each wave of sleepiness that crept up as the clock approached midnight was dissipated by the next sumptuous course: An intensely succulent leg of lamb. ("It's from Jean's farm," Annie said, gesturing toward the window as if the lamb lived next door. In fact, it had.) Braised baby vegetables from Annie's garden and garlic-stuffed artichokes with big, shameless dabs of butter. Wild rice with pomegranate and asparagus in a rich cream sauce. Five different cheeses. A caramelized *tarte tatin* laced with bitter chocolate and puff pastry.

I was a culinary virgin at the time, and with each high-fat, lactose-heavy, buttery bite, a little American voice inside me shrieked helplessly, *"You shouldn't! You can't! You've just consumed more calories in the last twenty seconds than in the last twenty years!"* But by the time the Armagnac was poured into lovely glass goblets, by the time the candles had burnt down into pools of smoldering liquid and the conversation, which covered everything from politics to pantomime, had veered off into a salacious discussion about the sex life of American politicians (which pales, by the way, in comparison to their French counterparts), I was either too drunk, too full, or simply too happy to care.

It is a cliché of almost monumental proportions to associate the French with food, and yet it is inevitable: Nowhere is respect for ritual more striking in French life than when it comes to food. An extravagant confluence of historical influences has put France on the gastronomical map as the undisputed leader in world taste, and graced the French girl with a legacy of exuberantly rich culinary and dining rituals. Food is culture. It is history. It is identity. It is pleasure. And it is savored with the same singular enjoyment as sex.

The Ritual of Dining

Food invariably brings out the best in the French and the worst in Americans. We Anglo-Saxons starve ourselves counting calories but what we're really craving is pleasure and ritual. Zen foodie Edward Espe Brown once declared

A *New Yorker* writer from the 30s and 40s, Liebling wrote this slightly dated but wonderful book about eating in Paris. "There would come a time," he once wrote, "when, if I had compared my life to a cake, the sojourns in Paris would have presented the chocolate filling. The intervening layers were plain sponge."

that enjoyment is one of the unacknowledged keys to eating wisely. The French girl knows this instinctively. Forget McDonalds or the advent of Starbucks-type cafés in Paris; the French girl does not live the take-out life. It is still almost impossible to get a coffee to go in France. You might see waiters rushing across tiny, traffic-filled streets carrying trays filled with porcelain demi-tasses of espresso to various local merchants—such is the privilege of being an integral part of a specific *arrondissement* and, more precisely, a specific street—but otherwise if you want to eat or drink on the run, you're in the wrong country. You will rarely see the French girl eating in her car, munching on the road, or snacking in a check-out line.

The French girl lives the sit-down, stay-seated, savor-every-bite life. Food anchors her in a collective ritual that is one of the backbones of civilization: the coming together over food, the baking and breaking of bread, the communion, the conversation. Dining together is almost a na-

"Dining is a solemn rite to the French because it offers the double opportunity of good eating and good talk. Everything connected with dinner-giving has an almost sacramental importance in France. The quality of the cooking comes first; but once this is assured, the hostess' chief concern is that the quality of talk shall match it."
EDITH WHARTON

tional religion, and at regular intervals you can almost hear the collective scrape of chairs as the French sit down to a meal at roughly the same time all over the country. Work life comes to a screeching halt. Heavy shutters clank shut like steel curtains as merchants retire for lunch breaks that, in some cases, can last up to three seriously gratifying hours. Sunday meals are often day-long affairs (and since everything is closed in France on Sunday, what else is there to do but eat?) and wine glasses are clinked together all over the country—*Santé!*—which is as close as the French get to saying national grace.

The ritual of food has even shaped the French meal itself: Just as the American meal reflects our Anglo-Saxon obsession with time (it's fast, functional, and all-on-one-plate), the French girl's meal reflects her own culture's obsession with time. She eats each course separately and makes fast food slow. ("I will *not* eat my salad *with* my burger," protested visiting French girlfriend Claudine at a local burger joint. She then proceeded to amuse her fellow diners by eating her hamburger with a knife and fork.)

The French girl's food sensibility is primed at a very early age. I had the experience of attending to three small French children (ages four through eight) while they ate lunch at their home without their parents. I was only asked to watch over them; the kids would take care of everything, the mother assured me. And they did. With exceptional grace and a certain poise that defied their age, they ate each course separately and with great care: from the grapefruit (pre-cut by *Maman* into tiny pulpy triangles, which they ate with a sprinkling of sugar) to the white bean and smoked ham *cassoulet* and the final cheese plate with figs. They ate with real cloth napkins and real glasses, and their cutlery was entirely adult. As I watched them eat like little apostles, images of space-age TV dinners in tin trays came back to haunt me from my own American childhood. How pious these children seemed in front of their well-prepared plates! How devoted to the savory implications of each bite!

The French girl grows up eating *à la française,* and everything in her life conspires against her eating any other way. Even her public school cafeteria features lovely well-planned four-course meals and a scrumptious dessert for all—unthinkably adult compared to American public-school fare. And the long pause between the end of her school day (4:30 P.M.) and her dinner (8:30 P.M.) is

Le Goûter

Around four o'clock every day, while the American girl is munching a grainy nutrition bar—or worse, a Snickers bar and a soda—the French girl is slipping into a nearby café for a sip of something hot and a nibble of something yummy. This is *le goûter*, a charming custom that's the French equivalent of English teatime. For children, it's a much-needed snack between the end of school and dinner (a *pain au chocolat*; a madeleine); for adults, it's a bit of tea or espresso or hot chocolate, a bite of baguette and butter topped with a shaving of bittersweet chocolate, or perhaps a macaroon. It is also a little time to breathe, to socialize, or to get lost in the pleasant commotion of a busy café in the company of oneself. As with all things food-related, in France *le goûter* is as much about rhythms and ritual as it is about sustenance.

punctuated by *le goûter*—something consistently delicious enough to hold her over until dinner but not too much to spoil her appetite.

Three Meals

A holy trinity, a sacred trio: Three meals a day anchor the French girl in ritual, support her careful habits regarding food, and give each meal a distinctive tenor. Her typical *petit déjeuner* consists of a sliced baguette with generous pats of real butter and homemade fruit preserves downed with a black coffee or a hot chocolate in a melon-sized saucer—eaten *en famille*. Because France is not a big breakfast culture, the French girl rarely eats a man-sized plate of eggs and bacon. Equally rare is the idea of a business breakfast: Unless you're en route to Hong Kong via Paris (in which case, you'll sit at an early breakfast with the bleary-eyed French), business almost always runs smoother with a glass of *grand cru* by one's side—and even the French are reasonable enough to resist the temptation before noon.

The French girl's lunch might be spartan (a *salade frisée*, fresh tomatoes and mozzarella) but it will often include bread and will end with a creamy triangle of Brie and a small square of dark chocolate. Her dinner will be eaten when most Anglo-Saxons are bedding down for the night, and it will usually involve wine, three courses, and a small dessert. (And, oh yes, the bread.) But the French girl will only eat three meals a day. No grazing, no scarfing down convenience food on the run, no metabolically mapped-out five small meals. And no snacking.

No Snacks, S'il Vous Plaît

One of the big faux pas made by American marketers of EuroDisney was the assumption, among other things, that the French would snack the way Americans do. *Mais non.*

When the theme park opened to big fanfare in France their concession stands, packed with sugared popcorn and shiny candy bars, were vacant.

Like the all-you-can-eat-buffet or drive-thru fast food, snacking is a uniquely American habit. The French girl simply does not snack. You will not find her standing in front of her fridge, pondering and picking away with that conflicted look of boredom, craving, and encroaching guilt. She doesn't graze through entire bags of nonfat, low-sodium, high-fiber crackers while waiting in the check-out line. She usually won't even eat popcorn at the movies. Or drink coffee and drive at the same time. Or struggle with the desire for instant gratification. She knows that like history itself, mealtime will repeat itself. If her stomach rumbles, she won't rush to its rescue; she holds out with the knowledge that the longer she waits, the sweeter the return.

By not snacking and savoring each course independently in a fully anticipated meal, the French girl gets some important side benefits: She can actually feel her body's hunger pangs and satiety cues. (Wolf down your food and you're never full, so you keep on eating.) Her gastrointestinal juices are happy, and they in turn break down her food better. She has a heightened sense of pleasure from each course. There may be multiple courses to a French meal, but the portions are modest (the size of a child's fist), not super-sized (the size of a linebacker's fist), and there are no second helpings, which helps explain why deluxe French meals don't do as much damage to the waistline as the average American meal.

After a particularly rich meal, or a weekend away with lots of eating and drinking, the French girl quickly, quietly and briefly compensates by scaling back for the next day or two. Water instead of wine, light meals with lots of fresh vegetables. This temporary adjustment keeps it all in balance, as it should be.

The truth about the high-pleasure, high-fat diet is that it has served the French girl well over the centuries. Simple pleasures probably never killed anyone, the French will argue, though lack of them can. When asked the secrets to her longevity, French centenarian Jeanne Calmont said, "Every day, a bit of chocolate and port wine." The French girl knows that it might be the champagne, *foie gras*, and chocolate—eaten with discretion, moderation, and enthusiasm—that actually keep her alive.

Only the Good Stuff

To the French, a meal consists of the best, truest components one can afford and dining consists of the best each party can bring to the experience—from food to conversation. Excellent quality underlies even the simplest meal, and this informs the French girl's approach to making and serving food.

One of the most practical considerations she faces is space. Like her closet, her refrigerator is positively puny

Her Friend Gitane

"None of the faint-hearted intercourse cigarette nonsense," the *Guardian* once wrote. "Jeanne Moreau smokes for Europe. She smokes with a spoon in one hand and a fag in the other, elegantly alternating her nourishment."

The French government has tried (feebly, but nonetheless) to curb the nation's appetite for *la cigarette*, but it remains as iconic as berets and baguettes. It's a habit and an accessory. So if you want to stay friends with the French girl, don't get between her and her cigarette. She knows it's not good for her, but that's her business. (Never mind that her second-hand smoke might end up *your* business.) And if you can't figure why they still puff away despite the Surgeon General, consider these problematic words of wisdom: Several years ago while pregnant in Paris, I asked a nurse why administrators were allowed to smoke in the maternity ward (yes, the maternity ward). After a moment's pause, she looked at me sternly. "Not letting people smoke would be an infringement on individual rights," she said, pretty much summing up the national consensus on the subject.

compared to the standard Buick-sized American version. But as with wardrobe, she does far more with much less, and with stupefying results. Her open markets thrive and flourish according to the seasons: The French girl cannot buy fresh cherries or peaches in the winter for example,

French Girls We Love

M.F.K. FISHER

For making us see the sensual and profound in food through her deliciously rich prose. M.F.K. Fisher may have been born a California girl, but she was totally French in her heart and soul and, most of all, in her palate. She lived, married, wrote, and ate in France for the better part of her life. Her world view, fine and graceful and elegiac, is matched by her style, which W.H. Auden called the best of the twentieth century.

She wrote of a time when La Tour d'Argent served "a mixed pie of snake, porpoise, swan, and plum-stuffed crane." She wrote of food and love, all with a rich and creamy Proustian flair. Fisher gave us a language for how to approach life, grabbing every grain of opportunity, just in case it might contain a bit of beauty or a fragment of truth: "I ate, with a rapt voluptuous concentration which had little to do with bodily hunger, but seemed to nourish some other part of me."

Read *A Considerable Town*, about Marseille, and *Map of Another Town*, about Aix-en-Provence, to share Fisher's profound appreciation of all things French. Read *The Physiology of Taste*, her brilliant and rousing translation of Jean Anthelme Brillat-Savarin's brilliant and timeless 1825 treatise on food and other matters of life and death. And read *The Art of Eating*, which is a collection of five of Fisher's books, and turns out to be about the Art of Living, of course.

or the best apples and pears in the summer. (In fact, she wouldn't even try.) Likewise she won't find fresh halibut on Monday if fishermen haven't reined in a good catch on Sunday. She knows the growing seasons and the vagaries of weather; she knows her local farmers, walks to the market regularly and shops for the day, not in bulk buying sprees. She will spend entire Sunday mornings at the farmer's market strolling through various stalls, examining the shiny flesh of an eggplant, the texture of new corn, the richness of a *chèvre*. She will pick through troughs of potatoes (pink, white, cream, and violet spuds of every shape), examine a marbleized flank of beef, sniff her way through bins of freshly baked Poîlane and cracked wheat breads. Maneuvering adroitly through caddy pile-ups along the way, she will push and shove her way if necessary to get her hands on the fresh cod that's "going, going fast, Mesdames, Messieurs!" and the little glass jars of honey and hand-milled soap from the eccentric beekeeper from Ardèche, then cruise through the hardware stall with its hanging baskets, steamers, kettles and sponges.

And in the end, she will not make a *cassoulet* if it's summer or a *salade niçoise* if it's winter—because she can't get the best ingredients for the season, because it doesn't make sense, and because there is a right moment for all things. She will make what is ripe, ready, flourishing—and she will often cook by hand, by smell, by scratch, using all of her senses in the making of her meal. Which is why when she comes to the States she admires the convenience of twenty-four-hour shopping, but still yearns for that seasonal tomato that is so ripe it's almost sentient. She longs for less choice and more quality; she spurns the refrigerated air, the suspicious-looking plastic-wrapped trays with out-of-season produce, and insistent glow that keeps everything in a space-age stasis. For the French girl the act of food shopping is part of a master plan that has united human beings and Mother Nature in an irrevocable quest for nourishment and pleasure. Anything else is just an errand, merely a chore.

When she finally makes her choices, the French girl works magic with what she gets on a daily basis and there is something spontaneous about her meal. She doesn't create a menu according to a rigid plan but according to what the natural cycles have in store for her: She plans for improvisation, and she improvises with her plan.

The proof of Martine's gift for choosing her foods is found in the way she prepares them. What's available, what's in season, and never from a cookbook (she reads cookbooks for fun, but rarely follows a recipe and always cooks from scratch). When it comes to quantities and measures, it's all "by eye, whatever looks and smells right . . ." A perfect example of Martine's free form cooking:

Martine's Duck with Fruit

Cook two fresh duck breasts, skin on, over medium heat, ten minutes on each side. Keep the pan juices and put breasts aside when done. Add a pinch of salt, pepper and a spoonful of honey and balsamic vinegar to the juices; then add some fresh peaches, fresh figs or fresh pitted

To Market with Martine

What does a demanding, gastronomically endowed French girl look for when she buys fresh food? Here are French girl-friend Martine's strict (and strictly sensual) requirements:

Tomatoes: They must be very red and very firm. Branch tomatoes have much better taste. I love the smell of their stems.

Lettuce: I never buy packaged lettuce, even when I'm in a big rush. Lettuce must be bought utterly fresh or it shouldn't be bought at all. When I buy it, I look at the heart of lettuce, that's where you have your secret: The leaves must be folded firmly together and they must be very light in color. If you see that in your lettuce heart, you buy it right away!

Carrots, celery and cucumbers: Never in plastic packages. Firm and very green for the celery and cucumbers, with an almost tangy scent. Carrots must be bought individually, never pre-packed, and the more dirt on them the tastier they will be.

Beets: I buy them cooked and stocked in big purple bins from my grocer. Again, never pre-packed and never canned—too sweet, no satisfying heft in the mouth.

Beans and peas: I prefer extra-fine string beans from Kenya or Morocco, and fresh peas only in the spring. They all must be very fresh of course, and have no little black spots on them.

Melons: Very heavy, with a ripe fruity scent. If their little stem comes off easily, they're perfectly ripe.

Plums and peaches: For plums, they must be as flush red as possible—some can be almost too ripe, while others must be

Continued on next page . . .

almost crunchy, depending on the variety. Peaches must be velvety and ripe, but not too ripe, and very fragrant: Sometimes they smell like roses. There are white peaches and yellow peaches. And they must never look the same. To each peach, its personality!

Apples and pears: Very crunchy, very flush with color, very fragrant. At the farmer's market I will visit each merchant who is selling apples and buy their particular variety. They are always good, never ever treated with chemicals or waxed. They have not been machine washed. Anything that is too 'clean' is lifeless. And that is not a good thing for the palate.

Cheese:

Reblochon: Must be extremely refined and is delicious melted on cooked potatoes.

Chèvre: There are dozens of sorts, and I love them all. I usually buy them not too dry, dusted with ash, and serve them in generous slices on small warm toasts in my salad.

Comté: Very, very fruity—more intense than a Gruyère and ultimately more satisfying.

Bleu or Roquefort: Must be very refined, buttery almost, and best served in a salad with fresh walnuts, endive and slices of firm, tart apple.

Meat: Good red meat is very pink and has an almost pearly quality to it. Poultry must be extremely firm and farm-fresh.

Fish: I almost always buy whole fish. First I look at the eyes: if they look almost alive, the fish is truly fresh. If the eyes seem glazed over or cloudy, I avoid it. The gills must still have a trace of blood; if the fish is already cut, it must smell like the ocean. If it smells like anything else—or worse, like nothing—I won't buy it.

Bread: Must be well baked, with a nice firm crust, not too white, and smell doughy.

cherries and cook over low heat. The fruit will slowly melt. Thinly slice the duck and add to the fruit/gravy mixture. Served with a purée of potatoes and celeriac.

The Fresh Rule

Eating food that is brimming with earthiness is also part of the French girl's culinary gestalt, and nothing will solicit more mockery at a French restaurant than popping a slew of vitamins with your meal. I know. Whenever my health-conscious mother would visit from California she'd bring along plastic baggies filled with monster-sized megavitamins, which she'd swallow with her meal to the derisive stares of French diners.

The French girl rejects the supplements and vitamin craze, and the reasoning goes something like this: "If you eat *fresh* foods, why would you need vitamins? Eat a real *fresh* orange for your vitamin C. Make some real *fresh* lentils for iron. Or put *fresh* spinach in your quiche."

Sounds sensible. Why pop vitamins when you can get the real thing in the recently harvested bounty of local farmers? Food is so fresh in local markets that she's accustomed to clods of dirt packed in sheaths of leeks or tiny insects embedded in lettuce leaves. If she's eating in the countryside, chances are high her meal is so fresh it was walking around on all fours just before she ate it. (Particularly troubling to vegetarians, who until recently were considered extraterrestrials in France.) And if her food began life in a petrie dish, she'll know about it, because

Europeans fanatically legislate the labeling of genetically-modified food (and rightly so). It's all a reminder that real fresh food comes from the soil, not from a factory. When my French neighbor, Martine, makes her outrageously delicious *foie gras* she doesn't go for the pre-cut, pre-wrapped livers in their little plastic trays. She buys a 700-gram, freshly-gutted free-range goose liver from her local butcher and de-veins the entire slippery, red organ on her kitchen table in what looks like a scene from a French emergency ward. "It tastes so much better this way," she says, entirely composed in her bloody cooking gloves. And so it does.

Urban or rural, the French girl is also a rapacious gardener. She's got a pot of basil growing on her sill, flowers on her patio, or a *potager* that she maintains in the country. A pair of well-worn gardening shoes, battered gloves, and a small beaten hoe are a permanent fixture in French country homes.

The Psychology of Shopping

The first time Corinne strolled the aisles of an American supermarket, looking a little lost and very overwhelmed, she asked in total earnest: "How many brands of breakfast cereal and potato chips do Americans need to be happy?" Here was a woman who was, of course, as svelte as they come, but who consumed food with relish and utter gusto. History had given her enough common sense to eat right and well, enough sensuality to embrace the buttery, high-fat foods that we Americans abominate, and

Borrow A Page From the French Girl's Book: Eating

Take time to eat. Be ritualistic about preparing, serving, and eating your food. Remember that food and ritual connect you to the world. Be sensual about food, not utilitarian. Eat modest portions of excellent food, never giant portions of anything. Eat well or not at all. Indulge in simple pleasures.

On Eating Out vs. Eating In

"French restaurants are for gluttons and gourmands," Frédérique loves to say. (She is thin as a rail but has an appetite the size of the Massif Central.) French cuisine in and of itself is extraordinary enough to inspire the natives to stretch their wallets (there is La Tour d'Argent and Lucas-Carton, among many others) or their culinary stamina (take Pharamond, for example, where you can feast on savory brains and tripe to your endless delight). But a stupendous number of restaurants cater to nearly every taste in France—and all of them are an opportunity for the French girl to travel vicariously and stray from the staples that make a regular appearance at her dinner table.

So while she might frequent a local haunt for a favorite regional specialty (*cassoulet* from the southwest, say, or sauerkraut from Alsace), ethnicity is often what she seeks when dining out. Post-colonialism has brought North Africa to her plate with heavenly spiced tagines and couscous, and Southeast Asia with innumerable Vietnamese specialties. She'll feast on feijoadas from Brazil or tabboulehs from Lebanon. There are borschts and caviar from Russia, paellas from Spain, stuffed carp from central Europe, and endless pasta dishes from her Italian neighbors. Her own cooking might be strictly French, but her palate is polyglot and global.

The Café

The café is iconic in the French girl's life. It is reassuring in its sameness over the centuries. (Sartre and de Beauvoir hung out at the Café Flore. So can you.) The French girl might come here to be alone. It might be her home away from home, where she catches up with herself or a friend or where she goes to steal a quiet moment to write a letter. There is no styrofoam here. No multiple sub-species of coffees. Nothing to-go. There is espresso in a real cup and saucer. And there is wine. And there is the lure—no, the imperative, the prerequisite—of the café itself, which is to provide a public space for the private self to endlessly linger.

enough self-control to manage the whole experience with natural ease and a guilt-free conscience.

Shopping in large American-style French supermarkets is on the list of the top ten most unpleasant experiences in France. The chronically long and disrespected lines, the heavy-bagged jostling, the lack of customer service— the French girl would rather avoid the whole thing entirely. Instead, she does a light daily marketing for just the right ingredients necessary to build a meal for the next day or so, or to restock on the essentials. If she sees something enticing—a fresh catch of cod, just picked apples from Calvados—she'll build her meal around that rather than stick to a prescribed plan.

Le Film

MILOU EN MAI
(May Fools)

This film by Louis Malle is as much about food as it is about family, which makes it doubly worth the viewing. A family gathers in the countryside for the funeral of the clan's matriarch. It happens also to be the time of the dramatic labor strikes of 1968 and the threat to the *bourgeois* way of life is very real. This film jumbles together the tension of the times with the crackling dynamic of a group of flawed but interesting people yoked by blood and history. See it for the great meals, great scenes, secrets, confessions, love, death—this film has it all.

In the Kitchen

Over the course of my years in France, I learned to make rich cheese tarts and indecently high-fat cakes. I learned how to de-vein a goose liver, properly stuff a chicken, and graciously tear lettuce—by hand, in big generous pieces, never chopped. I fussed with Fahrenheits and metric systems, and learned to shop with a Zenlike patience I never knew I had in me. And I learned it all from a quintessential French girl, who happened to be my neighbor.

Martine not only gave me my first primers on cooking and eating the French way; she also stripped me (or tried

What's in Her Pantry?

High-quality cold-pressed virgin olive oil, mustard, balsamic vinegar and assorted wine vinegars (the staples for vinai-grette), dried herbs and spices (tarragon, curry, cumin, *herbes de Provence*), pasta, fresh pistachios and high-end crackers for last-minute cocktails, sugar, flour, baking powder, yeast, vanilla and other baking staples, exotic pepper, coarse gray sea salt and *fleur de sel*, sugar cubes stacked in an ancient tin box (absolutely no artificial sweeteners), and homemade apple and berry preserves. A few tins of exceptional, high-quality *foie gras*.

Borrow A Page from the French Girl's Book: Shopping for Food

Don't shop as if it's a chore—make it a thoughtful part of your meaningful relationship with food. Make time to shop with a good butcher, cheese shop, produce market, fish market and wine shop. Find a local outdoor farmer's market and become a regular. Pick foods based on seasons, colors, textures. Let your senses do the shopping. Buy something you've never eaten and cook with it. Invest in a big, beauti-ful basket or colorful caddy so you can learn to shop on an intimate scale.

What's in Her Fridge?

The French girl's *frigo* is always stocked with some basic essentials for her own cooking or to receive unexpected guests for an impromptu *apero* (aperitif). She usually has on hand:

Fresh cream, salted butter*, milk, eggs, yogurt, mustard, grated fresh parmesan, a small piece of *chèvre* or mozzarella, a bottle of champagne, a bottle of bubbly water, anchovies, olives, tapenade, dark chocolate, fresh basil, parsley, chives, cilantro, thyme, and garlic. The tomatoes are stashed outside the fridge.

*Cheese is often left outside the fridge so it ripens and has a full robust taste. Ditto for butter, which is removed from the fridge one or two hours prior to use.

to anyway) of many engrained residual California habits. "You cannot serve a salad for a meal," she'd say. Or "Get to know and love your butcher no matter what his politics might be. Make food with your bare hands. Always use cast iron. Use only whole milk, real butter, pure sugar, and fresh cream. And never, ever eat standing up."

Not every French girl is raised to be a culinary goddess. But she is raised to value those basic principles regarding freshness and quality, and she makes sure she knows how to make a few simple things extremely, reliably well. An omelette, a vinaigrette, a piece of fish with herbs. This so she knows she can always feed herself well—or anyone

The French Market Caddy

The postcard version of Paris features a French girl balancing a charming straw basket from the crook of her arm, in which she's thrown a newspaper, a baguette, a bottle of wine, and a leek. But this basket, or *panier*, is a little like the beret—more a romantic idea we have of the French than a reality. The truth is she is more likely than not pushing or pulling a market caddy, the small wheeled carts seen everywhere on the streets of France.

Where I come from, caddies live on golf courses and no one can shop without a car trunk. In France, the caddy is everywhere and the French girl can't shop without one clattering along the cobblestones, filled with her daily shopping. What's in her caddy?

Certainly a baguette. Mineral water and a bottle of table wine; nearly ripe cheese; a couple of pieces of fruit; fresh eggs; greens for salad; sausages or chicken or skirt steak or fish, depending on what looks good; and fresh herbs.

she may honor with the pleasure of an impromptu invitation for a home-cooked meal.

The French girl is also careful to cultivate a few signature dishes for that one memorable meal—somewhat fancier recipes than her basic eggs or *salade*. Chantal has her *coq au vin* and her *tarte tatin*. Camille has her white bean *cassoulet* and her *pommes dauphinoises*.

Le Livre

MASTERING THE ART OF FRENCH COOKING
by Julia Child, Louisette Bertholle, and
Simone Beck

This book was first published in 1961, and not a single book on French cuisine has appeared since then to topple its number one position. Child, yet another American with a French soul, and her French coauthors introduced a whole new world of food to Americans. They made it accessible without "dumbing it down," because as Child wrote, "If you can read, you can cook." Instruction and recipes on every basic French technique and ingredient provide a handbook for becoming a true master . . . or mistress, in the case of the French girl. If you weren't lucky enough to have inherited this classic, look for the beautifully produced fortieth anniversary edition.

On the Table

Besides the carefully chosen guests around the French girl's table, there is an important supporting cast *on* the table. These are the foundation on which sit the artful courses that comprise the French meal. I'm talking, of course, about the wine, the bread, the cheese, and the coffee.

Simply Perfect Eggs

In France, eggs are more likely to be served for dinner than for breakfast. And how to make perfect eggs has been a French obsession for centuries. M.F.K. Fisher lovingly translated Brillat-Savarin's nineteenth-century recipe for perfect eggs.

My recipe, guaranteed to grip a man's vitals if served with hate, and to soothe him like pansy petals if set down before him with gentle love, varies somewhat with the supplies to hand, but is basically this, and, as will be evident, it is quirky:

    8 fresh eggs
    1½ cups rich cream (more or less)
    salt, freshly ground pepper
    4 tablespoons grated cheese, or finely minced fresh herbs,
    if desired

Break eggs into cold, heavy iron skillet, add cream and stir gently until fairly well blended. Never beat. Add seasoning (and/or cheese and herbs) just before serving. This takes about half an hour—poky, but worth it.

This concoction is obviously a placid one, never to be attempted by a nervous, harried woman, one anxious to slap something on the table and get it over with. Its very consistency, slow and creamy, is a deterrent to irritation, and if it were attempted by any female who deliberately planned to lean over it, once on its plates, and whang at her guests (for a lover, a husband, a father, or a child is indeed the guest of any woman who prepares the food they must eat), I would rather have my scrambled eggs turn into hard, fanged snakes and writhe away. I love this recipe, for its very gentleness, and for the demands it makes upon one's patience, and the homage it deserves from its slow tasting.

    From *An Alphabet for Gourmets* by M.F.K. Fisher

Le Vin

I did not grow up around wine or wine drinkers. Back then drinking wine was something you did if you were a) celebrating or b) French. During my ten years in France I learned only a small fraction of what there is to know about wine: I cracked (but barely) the appellation code, developed an unwavering fondness for *blanc cassis*, and was able to distinguish between a Vouvray, a Puilly Fuissé and a Sauternes. I learned which glass to use with which wine, and which wine to serve with which dish. I traveled through the wine-making Edens of the Rhône and Loire valleys, the Jura and Bercy. I learned what is self-evident to the French girl: That there's nothing that can't be settled, appeased, enjoyed or celebrated over a glass of wine or a bottle of vintage cru. Likewise nothing complements a simple meal better than a rich, full-bodied wine.

The French girl knows that good wine is not just for snobs or connoisseurs. It is a both a staple and a genuine gesture of appreciation for herself and her guests. It is introduced, discussed, sometimes applauded, even gossiped about later if disappointing. She makes it her business to know enough about it to enhance the pleasure of her dining experience—and what she doesn't know her good friend, the neighborhood vintner, can tell her. Good wine, good glasses, and advice from an expert—no French girl would be without them.

Martine's Gigot d'Agneau

Martine had mastered the complexities of French cooking entirely, completely—and in heels. Wearing a thick white apron thrown over work clothes she'd chop and mix and stir away in her tiny kitchen, making everything look so easy. Her signature dish, a *gigot d'agneau*, was so simple yet so potently delicious that it cured me, one cold Parisian winter, of a raging flu. "Everyone," she told me, "must know how to make a very simple *gigot*." And so they must.

    1 leg of lamb (approximately 5 lbs)
    6–8 garlic cloves
    5 tablespoons olive oil
    fine herbs, salt and freshly ground pepper
    8 whole garlic cloves
    12 small potatoes

Preheat oven to 400° F. Drizzle half the olive oil over lamb and rub with garlic. Sprinkle amply with fine herbs. Roast lamb in oven one hour. Drizzle potatoes with remaining olive oil. Season generously with salt, pepper and fine herbs, and carefully place potatoes and garlic around the lamb. Cook an additional thirty-five to forty minutes, or until lamb is medium rare. Transfer lamb to a serving platter when done. Continue roasting potatoes until browned. Place potatoes and garlic together with the lamb on the platter.

Martine serves this simple dish with fresh buttery green beans and braised fennel topped with fresh Gruyère and you're likely to weep when you eat it.

Le Film
BABETTE'S FEAST

This Academy Award-winning Danish movie, based on a story by Isak Dinesen, tells the story of Babette, a former Parisian chef of great renown who has taken refuge in Denmark in the home of an austere and religious Lutheran family. For twelve years, she works as their housekeeper and cook, careful to keep house and prepare food according to their simple, plain ways. When Babette comes into a sum of money, she convinces her benefactors to allow her to prepare them a special meal. The preparation of this gorgeous masterpiece of a meal is a study in itself, as is the magical effect it has on this gathering of rigid, humorless people.

Savor the menu of Blinis Demidoff, Quail en Sarcophage, Endive Salad, and Baba au Rhum. And see this movie of quiet beauty as an homage to friendship and food, and to art and grace.

Le Pain

There's a *boulangerie* on every corner in France for a good reason—the French love their bread and its absence from the table can have dangerous repercussions. Remember those bread riots in 1789 that presaged the French Revolution and caused Marie Antoinette to say, "Let them eat cake!"? Did someone say *guillotine?*

Blinis Demidoff

It turns out Isak Dinesen was just teasing us with the magical
dishes she invokes in *Babette's Feast*. She included no recipes, and only hints of what the dishes might really be. Below
is a faithful approximation of Dinesen's Blinis Demidof,
adapted from the recipe created by Chicago's Theater Oob-
leck for their stage version of *Babette's Feast*.

For the Blinis:
1 teaspoon active dry yeast
2 ¾ cups all-purpose flour
3 ¼ cups warm milk
4 eggs, separated
¼ teaspoon salt
Clarified butter

For the Topping:
4 medium beets, tops removed
¼ cup grated fresh horseradish (or 6 teaspoons prepared)
1 tablespoon cider vinegar
2 tablespoons freshly squeezed orange juice
½ teaspoon sugar
¼ cup grated ginger
1 cup grated carrots
Salt and pepper to taste
Sour cream
Chives

In a large bowl, mix together yeast, ½ cup of the flour and 2
cups of the milk. Cover and set aside at warmer than room

Continued on next page . . .

temperature for 30 minutes. Let the remaining milk cool at room temperature.

Beat the egg yolks and stir into the yeast mixture with the remaining milk and flour and ¼ teaspoon salt.

Beat the egg whites to stiff peaks and fold into the batter. Cover and let rest in a warm place to rise for 1 hour.

Meanwhile, cook the beets until tender in a large pot of boiling, salted water. Let the beets cool, peel, then grate beets and mix with the horseradish, vinegar, orange juice and sugar. Cool mixture in the refrigerator.

In a large skillet, sauté the ginger and carrots in clarified butter until just heated through. Season with salt and pepper and set aside to cool.

When cool, add ¾ cup carrot mixture to blini batter.

Heat a nonstick skillet over medium-high heat. Brush lightly with clarified butter and cook three blinis at a time, each 3 to 4 inches in diameter. Cook for 1 to 1 ½ minutes, then flip and cook the other side about 1 minute, until puffy and golden brown. Remove cooked blinis to a platter and keep warm while preparing remaining blinis.

Serve blinis warm, topped with a small dollop of sour cream and a spoonful of the carrot-beet mixture. Garnish with chives. Makes approximately 40 blinis or 12 to 15 servings.

Baba au Rhum

This is the sweet and comforting closer to the meal that left Babette's guests swooning.

    1 package yeast
    ⅓ cup warm milk
    2 ⅓ cups sifted flour
    3 tablespoons unsalted butter, softened
    2 ⅔ cups sugar
    6 eggs
    5 ½ cups water
    ½ cup dark rum
    Candied fruits or thinly sliced almonds for decoration

Dissolve yeast in milk in a large bowl. Stir in ½ cup of the flour, cover, and set aside in a warm place to rise for 30 minutes.

Beat 7 tablespoons of the butter in a food processor. Add two tablespoons of the sugar and 2 tablespoons of the flour. Then beat in the eggs one at a time.

Beat remaining flour into the risen yeast mixture, then beat in the butter and egg mixture to form a thick, doughy batter. Butter a large baba or Savrin mold (or bundt pan) with a tablespoon of butter, then spoon batter into the mold. Cover with a clean cloth and set aside to rise until dough reaches the top of the mold.

Heat oven to 350 degrees. Bake baba for 40 minutes, until golden brown on top.

Meanwhile, combine remaining sugar and water in a saucepan and boil until syrupy and reduced to about 3 cups. Remove from heat and stir in rum.

Continued on next page . . .

After baba is removed from the oven, spoon warm rum syrup over it entirely, allowing it to saturate the cake completely.

Let cake cool, then unmold and decorate with candied fruits or nuts before serving.

Serves about 8.

As with wine and cheese, the French are very strict about the business of bread. Laws require that in order to qualify as an authentic *boulangerie*, bread must be made from scratch on the premises. In other words, it's got to be fresh.

Lionel Poilâne, France's most noted baker, was famous for the savory bread that bears his name *miche Poilâne*, round loaves made from stone-milled flour. This bread is rich and thick and dark—and authentically French. This in contrast to the baguette, which is light and white and fluffy, and, he claimed with a sniff, actually originated in Austria!

On bread, every French person has an opinion, a passion, a preference. So whether it's the beloved baguette or the hearty, rustic *pain de campagne*, the French girl makes sure there is daily fresh, excellent quality bread (and real butter) to accompany every meal.

Le Fromage

Charles de Gaulle once asked, "How can one be expected to govern a country with two hundred and forty-six cheeses?" It was a very good question. French cheese is a lot like the French themselves: The result of a convergence of elaborate traditions, complex regional tastes, and a certain charmed inclination toward eccentricity that can create surprising results. The French girl's stand on cheese is like everything else in her life: It must be authentic and high quality. (If it can be sprayed from a can or peeled out of plastic, it's not really cheese.) It must take time to make and eat. (Years for the former, hours for the latter.) It must be chosen carefully at least and creatively at best. And it must be a sensual experience of the most pungent, even tactile sort.

We Americans are likely to be too full for cheese at the end of a typical American meal. The French meal, by comparison, is so perfectly paced and proportioned that it begs for the bit of excitement an interesting cheese can bring in near the end. No French kitchen is complete without cheese ripening on a plate, chilling on a windowsill, or wrapped in thick lined paper in the refrigerator. And if you want to shock the French, try serving cheese *before* the meal rather than after it.

Le Café

A giant cup of rich coffee with steamed milk in the morning and a final cup (no milk) at the end of dinner—these are the Good Morning and Amen to a day filled with gastronomic pleasures. The French girl observes the simple rituals of coffee with care. She uses the best coffee—usually ground fresh in a shop that features an authentic five-foot brass coffee roaster—and made in the classic French press coffee pot. Whole milk gently steamed on top of the stove. Real sugar or none at all. Good oversized ceramic cups or bowls without handles for breakfast, antique china demitasse for dinner.

The trick is not thinking of coffee as a fix, like it's the jumper cables attached to your day. Instead, it's about taking the time for the pleasure of a fine, thoughtfully prepared cup, alone or with family and friends.

Borrow A Page from the French Girl's Book: Food

Be a food snob. If you're making a simple meal, make sure you have at least one outstanding item: an excellent vintage wine. A superb dessert. Know one recipe you can execute perfectly. Always be prepared to whip up an impromptu cocktail. Improvise according to the beauty and seasonal life of food.

Bake bread *en famille*. Break bread *en famille*. Cook by hand, from scratch. Use all of your senses when you cook. Become familiar with the basic beauty of flour, water, eggs, sugar and salt. Be religious about family dinners. Turn off the TV. Don't answer the phone. Talk about what you're eating. Converse. Ask questions. Put your utensils down while you eat. Savor.

What's On Her Table

While the French girl might go to theatrical heights of pageantry in displaying her fondness for *l'art de la table*, simplicity and taste usually dominate her table. If she's a purist, she might prefer fine matching porcelain with engraved flatware, crystal glasses and a beautiful linen tablecloth. If she's on the bohemian side, she delights in mismatched ceramics (called *faïence*) and a piece of decorative fabric from a flea market as a tablecloth. Or she may simply prefer the rustic pine of her exposed table, with its dark grainy fissures.

You'll certainly see bits of her history turn up on the table, maybe old linen napkins her grandmother embroidered at the edges or heirloom silver. There are flowers and candles and goblets for wine and water for guests, or simple tumblers for everyday. Oh, and a simple straw basket or elegant bowl (in pewter, glass, or wood) for *le pain*.

French Girls We Love
CHEF HÉLÈNE DARROZE

While French haute cuisine has always been a man's world, there is one Michelin star-winning woman chef. *Tout Paris* talks about Hélène Darroze, who opened her eponymous restaurant in the Saint-Germain-des-Prés district in October 1999. Before that, her restaurant in Villeneuve-de-Marsan in the Landes in southwestern France had won the coveted Red Guide star. Food writer Patricia Wells points out the particular strengths of a woman chef, when she describes Darroze: "Like most fine female cooks, she offers more than just a sheer technical rendering of ingredients. She has a point of view, her food has depth, a definite warmth."

Caution: Just reading about her specialties is apt to cause swooning. Wouldn't it be worth a flight to Paris to taste Wood Fire Grilled Langoustines with Fresh Basque Baby Fava Beans and Slivers of Serrano Ham? Or Tomatoes Stuffed with Black Truffles and Confit? Or Grilled Foie Gras with Caramelized Fall Fruits and Porto Wine Reduction? Or Young Farm Pigeon stuffed like a "Poule Au Pot" with Creamy Foie Gras Sauce? Or Tarte Brûlée with Coconut and Roasted Pineapple, Passion Fruit Sorbet and Coconut Milk Caramel?

Fin

Ten years and innumerable French meals later, the little harpies in my head still occasionally warn of impending

"She died with a knife in her hand in the kitchen, where she had cooked for fifty years, and her death was solemnly listed in the newspaper as that of an artist."

Janet Flanner, writing about Mother Soret of Lyon. Soret's Chicken in Half Mourning was famous in France.

doom if I eat something too rich or too sweet, though they're a lot less pleasure starved than they were in my pre-France days. The French girl loves food—sometimes fanatically. She loves growing it, making it, and, most importantly, eating it. She experiences life largely through the pleasures of her palate. And she has taught me what M.F.K. Fisher meant when she wrote of eating ". . . with a rapt voluptuous concentration which had little to do with bodily hunger, but seemed to nourish some other part of me."

There are few better expressions of the French girl's essential qualities than when it comes to food: The time she spends and satisfaction she gets in the sensual making-and-eating-of. The insistent quality and discretion that informs every ingredient, each gesture, every bite. The stubborn traditions that give everything a certain reassuring yet exhilarating delectability. And the outrageous chefs, epicureans, and *bon vivants*—not to mention the generations of cooking mothers—who anchor everything in history. Food shapes the French girl, and she, in turn, is shaped by food. Empires may come and go, but there will always be *la cuisine*.

Five

La Fête

My first New Year spent in France went something like this: The preceding month of December was spent fêting the holidays with friends and family all over Paris and the French countryside. Parties, dinners, lunches, cocktails. Like everyone else, I ate enormous quantities of *foie gras*, as well as certain meats that tasted magnificent until I knew what they were, like *andouillette*, or blood sausage. We drank endless bottles of champagne and Bordeaux, and stayed up so late that it was the norm that month to be ending our revelry as the cock crowed at dawn in a distant field.

When January 1st rolled around, I breathed a sigh of relief. Time to repent. Time to make resolutions. Time to exercise restraint. Until January 6th, that is, when *la Fête des Rois* (the Feast of Kings) is celebrated on Epiphany, and obliges the French (and me, by default) to buy a large, almond frangipane cake from the local *boulangerie*, cut a hearty slice, and hope to find the tiny figurine of a king deep in its custardy center. The *Fête des Rois* was originally a very religious holiday dating back to the fourteenth century honoring the day it was believed the Three Kings arrived in Bethlehem. Now it is the occasion for family reunions and that amazing cake. When asked why they celebrate the *Fête des Rois* with such gusto, particularly so soon after fêting like mad the month before, most French people will shrug. "Any opportunity to have a party and eat cake," is how one French friend put it.

Indeed, beyond *la Fête des Rois* there are as many classic French *fêtes* as there are French girls, from the smoky stand-up cocktail that fills an industrial space or a private home with the din of clinking glasses and laughter, to the formal Communion party or pheasant-with-all-the-fixings Christmas buffet, with its ornate table settings and deeply comforting chestnut aromas. What binds together all this heady communal trysting and socializing is the collective focus on food and drink—so naturally the *soirée* that typifies the French *fête* par excellence is the dinner party.

The Dinner Party

The classic French dinner party might exude all the warmth of a Chardonnay commercial but it rarely has the drop-in, more-the-merrier backyard hospitality of the typical American party. That's primarily because the politics of space has everything to do with the politics of privacy: The smaller the space, the more intimate the experience. Everything in the French girl's world is on a smaller, more human scale, and this intimacy is something the French girl chooses. And it's something she navigates all the time. So like a little cameo wrought in furious detail on the tiniest piece of enamel, the French girl packs the most elaborate party into even the most cramped apartment, and the ambiance is intimate as much by design as by necessity.

One of the keys to the French girl's dinner party success is that she's both extremely well prepared and entirely committed to her own pleasure. A dinner party isn't a task; it's a process. She invests herself in its planning and preparation, so that when the party begins she's firmly at the helm but she's also cruising. The French girl may spend all day preparing—designing her meal around local fare at her open market, strolling through damp cellars filled with vintage wines, fretting at her local *fromagerie* over colossal rounds of St. Nectaire or Tomme de Savoie that will be perfectly ripe by that evening (not

What She Wears to Her Dinner Party

A black dress—her perfect little black dress—or perhaps silk palazzo pants with a silk blouse or tee. An understated but excellent piece of jewelry. If the gathering is more casual, she might wear jeans with heels and a simple black pullover. Tailored black slacks with croc loafers and a crisp white blouse. For the *bohème* or *excentrique*, maybe a vintage Japanese kimono over a tight black skirt.

by that afternoon, or by the following day). The preparation itself is part of the sensual, tactile process: She'll chop, dice, mince, roll, pound, pinch and stuff, with a glass of wine by her side and her favorite music in the background. There must be plenty of time for preparation, and it must be a pleasure, or it must not be at all.

She has left time for a bath. She emerges for the final minutes before her guests arrive with a refined, relaxed confidence.

As her guests amble in, stepping into the warmth of her home, shedding coats and purses, the French girl makes introductions with her trademark discretion: A brief introduction, never a full biographical blow by blow. (You'll never hear her say, "Hi, meet Pierre. He's a lawyer who lives in the seventeenth *arrondissement,* just got a promotion and, guess what? He's single!") The French girl has chosen her mix of guests with care and you can expect her later to turn conversation to Pierre and his most recent case at just the right moment. *That* is how we get to know Pierre.

The French girl's guest list would consist of a few close friends or relatives, maybe a couple who she's getting to know better, perhaps an associate or two from work, and, of course, Pierre, a new face and the companion of one of her guests.

You won't find any children present at the traditional French dinner party, and it's always a little shock when a child wanders into the room, rubbing his or her eyes and requesting *maman.* Dinner parties usually begin when the children are in bed and the intention is that they stay there. A mother's helper is sometimes enlisted to tend to children during the *soirée.*

The French girl will first offer her guests (what else?) champagne, which has been the libation of choice in France for thousands of years, along with a round of hors d'oeuvres: *petits fours* that she either spent hours making herself or that she bought at the best *patisserie.* (Either way they're heavenly.) There might be olives or tapenade. Caviar or *foie gras* and toast. A salty, slightly bitter cheese tart with delicate, homemade buttery crust. The French girl never puts her hors d'oeuvres in a desolate little corner or on a coffee table, expecting guests to partake self-service-style; she walks them around to each guest—*servez-vous*—at least once, if not twice, and no one refuses.

French Girls We Love
MADAME CLICQUOT

For being the mother of champagne. Widowed in 1805 at the age of 27, Nicole-Barbe Ponsardin Clicquot took over her husband's champagne company. She turned it into the prestigious House of Veuve Clicquot (*veuve* means widow in French), whose champagne is still the hallmark of special occasions today. The best of the best of her efforts is represented in Veuve Clicquot Grand Dame prestige cuvée, named after the widow herself. This wine is produced only in the finest years, and in limited quantities, and was once shared just with Madame Clicquot's family and closest friends. If anyone ever offers you a sip of this champagne, take it.

The aperitif is an important preamble—an extended moment for the warming of social juices; a slow-burning co-mingling of guests that reveals inklings of who each person is, a hint of political persuasions or cultural leanings, a little glimmer of personal passion that stirs enough curiosity to carry over to the dinner table. This moment is a little like foreplay and nothing can ruin the mood more than the inquisitions of an overly zealous partygoer who jumpstarts this collective courting with the invasive, "So, what do you do for a living?" That kind of American icebreaker is a hapless faux pas in France.

Because who you are in France is often more important

Les Petits Fours

As an hors d'oeuvre or with tea, the French girl serves these delectable little bite-size cakes. If they're served with tea, they are always nicely decorated with small pastille candies, sliced almonds, candied citrus zest, crystallized edible flowers and leaves, piped melted chocolate, or fresh berries. If you're served *petits fours* as an hors d'oeuvre, it will likely be salty and include a bit of cheese, olives, smoked salmon, or herbs. *Petit four* means "little oven," and the name originates from the small ovens used for baking the treats in the eighteenth century. If you order *petits fours* at a *patisserie*, you may find yourself eating any of a variety of rich cookies, including *cigarette russe, langue de chat,* or *miroir,* because the French use the term *petits fours* for both the cakes and the specialized small cookies. If someone serves you homemade *petits fours,* consider yourself a treasured guest.

that what you do for a living (never mind that we Americans can't seem to separate the two), it's not uncommon to spend a long evening with a dinner party guest and never learn what they do for a living. You may end up knowing, on the other hand, about their political ideology, the latest novel they read, or any number of steadfast and fervent opinions.

The aperitif can sometimes last up to an hour as the French arrive fashionably late and champagne bottles get emptied, lubricating the collective appetites not just for food but for conversation. The French girl, in the meantime, has an inner timer, a well-honed instinct that tells her when the moment is perfectly propitious to move on to the dinner part of the party. At which point she'll ask, "*On passe à table?*" And so they will.

The French girl is more concerned about seating people according to social interest than to social status, and creating chemistry means making sure that people with certain affinities find themselves literally rubbing elbows or facing off *tête-à-tête*. She also respects girl/boy seating arrangements at all costs, a "malicious little taboo" according to Wharton, but important to the French girl.

Somehow, miraculously, the French girl has made sure that while she's hostessing the aperitif, she also manages to slip off and check on dinner. She has orchestrated her preparations so that as much as possible is done well ahead of her guests' arrivals and all that's left is removing a dish from the oven or the carving of a roast, arranging a serving platter or a quick sauté of *haricots verts*.

Her meal begins with a starter, such as a *velouté de poireaux* or a vegetable tart. This is followed by her *pièce de résistance*, which is always a reflection of the season. If it's winter it might be a casserole-roasted veal with mushrooms and braised vegetables or a lamb stew with sauteed leeks and shallot vinaigrette. If it's summer it might be poached cod with lemon sauce and sun-dried tomatoes or stuffed artichokes and roasted salmon. A few bottles of excellent wine (previously uncorked so they

Le Film
CHOCOLAT

This is an English movie set in France, filmed by a Swedish director with notable English and American actors—and French girls Juliette Binoche and Leslie Caron. Binoche, who plays chocolatier Vianne, and Caron, who plays her widow neighbor, are one of the reasons to see this savory fairy tale of a film. They are each distinctly the picture of French womanliness.

The other reason to see this movie is for the sublime birthday dinner party Vianne throws for her landlord. Oh, the glowing candlelight. The long, rustic table draped in white. The roast chicken drenched with mole sauce, among other chocolatey indulgences. And the rapturous pleasure on the faces of her guests. This movie makes you want to have a dinner party, French style, right now. It also makes you want to dance, read poetry, sketch, fall in love, and, of course, nibble a chocolate truffle.

breathe), a basket of warm bread and a carafe of water are staples on her table.

[A moment to contradict myself: I once attended a dinner party that focused exclusively on razor-thin slices of nutty truffles eaten on toasted and lightly buttered Poilâne bread, and a bottle of vintage Bordeaux. The entire dinner, in all its simplicity, was grandiose.]

There might be a salad of baby greens with fresh herbs. And then there is, of course, the cheese, which is ceremoniously presented and eaten at the end of the meal af-

Serving Style

You will rarely see buffet-style service at the French girl's dinner party. The buffet is reserved for large cocktail parties or perhaps a garden party with many guests.

Presentation is paramount, though it's often done without an air of pretension. The French girl brings each course to the table, beautifully arranged with little aesthetically pleasing accents like fresh herbs or lemons, on a serving dish or platter. Every guest takes in the beauty of the dish, oohs and ahs from all.

She goes around the table and serves each guest, then sets it on the table or in the kitchen. She may also serve from a sideboard in the case of soup or salad.

Each course is served and eaten separately (there was a time when guests would rinse their mouths with water between courses from little bowls) and never rushed. Her family's old Limoges and silver might be used, or a collection of ceramics she bought in Italy or Spain. Dishes are changed with each course (dinner parties for old buddies being the exception, when there is sometimes debate over whether to change plates for the last round of cheese). Time is taken between each course, to clear away what's finished but more importantly to rest a bit before the next. This relaxed pace is good for the digestion and good for the hostess, who wants to move gracefully from course to course, while still spending plenty of time at the table enjoying the meal and conversation.

She may allow a family member or very close friend to help serve or clear dishes between courses, but never a guest whom she's just getting to know. She also doesn't accept help

Continued on next page . . .

from guests with clean-up after dinner—no big-group dish-wash-athons for her. The kitchen is her private mess. One wouldn't check out what's going on behind the curtain at the theatre, nor should one meddle in the French girl's kitchen at a dinner party.

ter the salad (but *before* dessert) and is often a *chef d'oeuvre* unto itself: big dusty gray cones of goat cheese, long unctuous slices of Brie de Meaux, pockmarked triangles of blue-veined Roquefort. The cheese plate is passed and each person uses a knife to cut a small portion of cheese to place on his own plate before handing it off to the next guest. Cutting cheese without holding it or letting it fly off the plate is no small task, and I had a few "cheese incidents" myself before mastering this fine art.

Dessert is often a gourmet delicacy (a crème brûlée or berry tart), either homemade or brought in, and is never declined by anyone. Calorie-counting at the French dinner party is like trying to breathe underwater (it just doesn't work) and excusing yourself with "I'm on a diet" is personal to the point of rudeness. Dessert is eaten in small portions and savored by all. It's followed by a *tisane* (a lemony verbena or citronella tea, often brewed with real herbs) or a coffee, and a cognac or brandy.

Le Menu For Dinner Party

STARTERS
Olives & tapenade
Petits fours
Small toasts with goat cheese, tomato and herbs

CHAMPAGNE
Veuve Cliquot

MAIN COURSE
Grilled sea bass with white butter sauce and chervil
Puff pastry filled with braised leeks and fennel
Steamed baby artichokes with summer vegetable paté

WINE
Sauternes blanc and/or Pouilly Fuissé

SALAD
Lambs lettuce, oak leaf, endive and arugula with a simple
vinaigrette

CHEESE
Cantal, Brie and chèvre

DESSERT
Black and white chocolate tart with red berry coulis and thin
almond pastry

DIGESTIF
Black coffee

Le Film

RIDICULE

This utterly entertaining movie, set in the late eighteenth century, really shows how much of a premium the French put on wit and clever conversation. It takes place in the Court of Louis XVI, where courtiers, social aspirants, and other hangers-on gather at one party or another, playing games and hoping for the opportunity to display their sparkling wit. This wit is not just light wordplay—it's a dangerous game the characters engage in at their own risk. Indeed, the wit of one turns against another, and fates and fortunes are determined by the outcome.

The party scenes are lush in period detail—bored rich people in powdered wigs, jockeying for the slightest edge in court society. Fanny Ardant is wonderful as the wickedly scheming Madame de Blayac. (Plus, she makes a compelling case for the deep and knowing beauty of an older woman versus the sweet but uninformed beauty of dewy youth.) We learn from her in no uncertain terms that one needs to say something cleverly or not at all, which may explain why the French girl is so careful about what she says and to whom.

Smart Talk

"There is no conversation more boring than the one where everybody agrees," Michel de Montaigne once said. Lively, intelligent and often provocative conversation is the lifeblood of the French girl's dinner party. Guests expect (and come prepared for) verbal engagement on almost any subject, although unless it leads to a general discussion about politics or culture, conversation about work life is not hot on the dinner party agenda. The French girl expects that guests bring their opinions, wit, and intellect to the table, and leave their work life behind.

Danielle lived just off the Trocadéro in the Left bank. Her home, an opulent eighteenth-century bazaar that represented every Louis under the sun and bric-o-brac from countless antique dealers, also featured a grandiose view of the Eiffel Tower. One doesn't ask how people like Danielle come to live in such a spread (one assumes inheritance, old money, good fortune), one only enjoys it, immensely.

We'd come together to loosely fête the arrival of the new millennium, which was toasted with a two-hour champagne fest (le Mums Cordon Rouge). The crowd was a slightly clannish group of friends and cronies: There was Antoine, lover of Bertrand, who was once the lover of Catherine, whose husband was, at present, with Agathe. There was a painter and gold-leaf expert. A prolific but unpublished writer of mysterious Slavic descent. A film director just back from Africa with a coterie of admiring assistants. There was a cello maker and a banker, and a foreign correspondent back from a distant war (whose tales of chasing Lady Di dominated the table before conversation splintered in a hundred directions) and a philosophy professor. Among others.

With intimate couplings in separate clusters of flamboyantly upholstered furniture in the cavernous salon, the party was not a whole but an ensemble of smaller parts; little groups of people in constellations of private discussion, sudden uproarious laughter, conspiratorial head nodding, and billows of smoke. Hostess Danielle moved from one group to the other; throwing her small frame into a plush chair nearly twice her size, crossing her legs into what looked like one braided body part, leaning forward with drink in hand and nodding in wry, passionate agreement before moving onto the next group. Meanwhile, a roving black-skirted Portuguese helper graciously offered plates of caviar, *petits fours* with salmon eggs and elaborately cut *crudités*—raw radishes meticulously carved like blooming tulips; carrots spliced into razor-thin spirals. Under the main table was a vestige of the aristocratic nineteenth-century past: a wire and button that, when pressed with the foot, summoned the *servantes*. (The French no longer use buzzers to summon their *domestiques*, but they still need the help.)

The Eiffel Tower was a majestic third presence at the table, filling one side of the room behind a nine-foot double-paned window with its stately, vaulting, bejeweled presence. (If you had any doubt where you were, you had simply to look out the window.) I counted six *grands crus* at the table when the meal began and stopped counting by the time the main course—a *magret de canard* with fresh figs, star anise, and tender white asparagus tips— was served. The conversation, which continued in animated clusters around the table, covered Gérard Depardieu's latest movie, the President of the Republic, the

American presence in Europe, a scandalous, recently released best-seller, tax reform, the politics of male ballerinas, the plight of African filmmakers, social welfare, and Hollywood. The conversation was pitiless, aggressive, cynical and whimsical. It was a sport, bulls heading off, horses at starting gates let loose with short reins. One of the objectives of Danielle's parties was not so much the meal itself but the people present at the table and their collective energy—refined but chaotic, animated and fashionably argumentative. In the preface to *At Home in France* Marie-Hélène de Rothschild speaks of French entertaining: ". . . however rich or poor one is, certain ingredients are essential: a pinch of madness, two dashes of refinement, three grains of effort—and a few heartbeats."

By the time the third course arrived the sky had turned a gauzy white and seemed to be spinning. Too much wine? No . . . snow! Conversation hushed as we watched the snow tumbling silently in feather-soft spirals and elegant loops against the tower. It was all so exquisitely French: At once imposing yet familiar, a beautiful thing

"She could dominate a room from a footstool . . ."
DIANA VREELAND ABOUT PAULINE DE
ROTHSCHILD

that was utterly impractical yet impossible to live without. While we'd come to toast the imminent new millennium, there was not the fervor you'd anticipate in the States. "Another millennium," one guest sighed. "We've gone through one before." Everyone nodded and took one last moment of reprieve before the party, like the snow, continued into the night.

The French Girl à la Fête

When the French girl fêtes, she's got her best stuff out there. As a guest, she's dressed with distinction. Conversation is a place where knowledge and charm converge. She never phones in her appearance at a party—she's invested in her own pleasure and in the impression she makes on others. The fête is an opportunity to flex her femmes, to catch a whiff of fresh air in the form of new acquaintances (especially men), and to catch up with friends and family.

As a hostess, all of the French girl's essential qualities

French Girls We Love
CATHERINE DE MÉDICIS

For exhibiting the qualities of a true Renaissance girl: an appreciation for art and architecture and a statesmanlike influence during the religious wars. Never mind she was born in Italy; Catherine, as Balzac wrote, "put forth the rarest fine qualities" and "saved the throne of France." In an effort to keep both Catholics and Huguenots on their toes, she sponsored lavish fêtes at the Royal Palace of Fontainebleu, importing Italian artists, poets, and even the first ballet, to the French court. Rumored to have asked her cobbler to fashion the first high-heeled shoe, Catherine loved spectacle as much as the next sixteenth-century girl; but when she staged a party, she was doing business. Read Balzac's biography of her, *Catherine de Médicis*.

come into play at her party: Her discretion informs all of her choices, from the inception of the party itself (whom to invite, what to serve, how to arrange the seating for excellent chemistry) to the food and conversation. But it's her show and she's the composer. She's taken all the time in the world to elaborate the nuances of her fête, with only quality in mind. This is reflected in her attention to the tiniest details, from the flowers on the table to the chill of the champagne.

Nobody is rushed, particularly the French girl herself. The sensual ambiance at the table—the intimacy of guests clustered closely around a table brimming with fragrant,

> ## *Borrow A Page from the French Girl's Book: Entertaining*
>
> Think of the party you are planning as a painting. You pick the scene, you pick the subjects, you pick the colors. Take the time to fill in all the details that will bring sensual pleasure to your guests and yourself. Don't bite off more than you can chew. Do only what you can do extremely well and with enough ease that you can enjoy yourself. Make time to relax and put yourself together before your guests arrive. Wear what feels good and makes your body happy. Tap into the chemistry of all your guests. Flirt. Do the dishes tomorrow.

warm food; the steam and smoke, the whole voluptuous tenor of it all—and the liveliness that comes with raucous, intelligent conversation, makes the French girl's dinner party intensely gratifying.

The sign of a successful French fête? Nobody leaves. It's well past midnight. Butts are spent. Wine bottles are empty. And you can almost hear the distant rumble of garbage trucks before the sated and exhausted guests part ways.

The Cocktail

The cocktail party is usually a lighter, more flexible affair than the dinner party. It's about stand up and mingle socializing, not sit down and be served. The cocktail party doesn't mind if its seams stretch a little as guests bring a

Le Livre

AT HOME IN FRANCE: EATING AND
ENTERTAINING WITH THE FRENCH
by Christopher Petkanas

This book is a tasty portrait of the dinner party *à la française*.
The author, who has lived in France for more than twenty
years, invites us into eighteen French homes in various
regions to distill the intimate art of French entertaining. By
steeping us in the "atmosphere of care, respect, and attention that is all the more engaging for being automatic," Petkanas helps us discover that the best hostess truly is relaxed
and at ease. That's his key to *l'art de recevoir*: the art of entertaining.

guest or two of their own. It's not about the food, although
wonderful and satisfying food is always served. It tries to
contain itself to a few hours, but it too can be guilty of
spilling smokily over into the next day. There's music,
there's ambience, there's conversation, there's chemistry—the French girl *loves* a cocktail party.

Le Mariage

The French girl's wedding is a fête of a different color,
usually an elegant shade of white. It doesn't much resemble our American break-the-bank, reception-hall extrav-
aganzas, but is a more intimate, close-knit affair. The
French girl's wedding usually features fewer guests,

The Kir

I once attended a party where Kir was the only drink served. It was a spontaneous early evening gathering of ten or so people. The food was simple—Agathe had picked up some unctuous cheese, salty tarts and fresh bread on her way home from work. And instead of fretting over stocking a bar for ten different tastes on short notice, she just served the Kir, love it or leave it. I happen to love it.

Champagne is irrepressibly grown-up and among my favorite libations. But a Kir is one of those lovely delicious little indulgences you allow yourself every day, any day. It's a drink you discover at a certain age: You are not past your prime, but you're usually way past twenty. The best Kir has a certain happy, syrupy glisten to it, a lightly fruity but no less substantial lift to it. When you sip a Kir, the glass is always half full.

The Kir is a simple concoction comprised of crème de cassis (a blackcurrant liqueur), dry white wine, and a twist of lemon. Crème de cassis (and the Kir) hail from Dijon, in the heart of the Burgundy region, where the same soil and climate that produces the fine wines of Burgundy also produces blackcurrants that are intensely rich in flavor.

Combined with dry white wine, such as White Burgundy Aligote, the crème de cassis becomes a Kir, a light and perfectly refreshing, crowd-pleasing cocktail.

To mix a perfect Kir:

Pour ¾ of an ounce (1½ tablespoons) of crème de cassis into a wine glass, fill with dry white wine, and garnish with a twist. To create a Kir Royale, use champagne instead of white wine. This drink is best served very cold.

French Girls We Love
EDITH PIAF

For immortalizing the People's Paris with her gigantic little voice. Legendary French chanteuse Edith Piaf sang on the streets as a teenager but eventually became one of the hardest working and most popular singers of her day. Fans who knew not a word of French were transported by the sheer artistry and great passion of her music, which did little to hide the tragic overtones of her life. To this day, "The Little Sparrow" epitomizes an emotional truth about France—and about life itself.

Go to the Musée Edith Piaf, a small private museum tucked in a working class neighborhood in Paris, where you can see many of her personal belongings, including furniture, a china collection and several of her tiny black dresses. And get carried away at your next dinner party by "La Vie en Rose," her signature song, on *The Voice of the Sparrow: The Very Best of Edith Piaf.* "Hymn à l'Amour," indeed!

fewer attendants (or none at all), and more attention to quality, tradition, and authenticity.

On the morning of her wedding day, the French girl's groom calls for her and they visit the neighborhood *mairie* to sign the civil marriage documents. From there, the betrothed pair make their way to the local church or to the town hall (preferably on foot, with a long line of well-wishers and little mismatched flower girls in tow). Or the ceremony may take place in the garden of her family's

What She's Wearing to Her Wedding

Eccentrics notwithstanding (there is always the wild French wedding that defies convention), the French girl is almost certainly not wearing an overwrought department store confection. She is wearing something refined but understated. Her dress is beautiful, but it did not cost a fortune—it is perfectly appropriate to her means and personal style. It is white or ivory, but not too frou-frou, perhaps a dress she inherited from her grandmother and will pass on to her daughter. Or it may be short, even sexy. She might wear it again to a cocktail party.

As with her day-to-day style, she is careful but purposeful with her accents—a hint of an heirloom necklace or earrings, a delicate simple veil if any. Her flowers are a relaxed bouquet of seasonal blooms—she may even have picked them herself. Her hair is in a classic style, perhaps swept back in a *chignon*, and her makeup is subtle. And she does her hair and makeup herself, *merci beaucoup!*

Her groom, by the way, is wearing an excellent dark suit or tasteful, low-key black tie. There are no matching outfits among attendants—all are trusted to use their own good taste when getting dressed for the day!

country home. Or in a jewel of a seventeenth-century *château* in a tiny hamlet deep in the French heartland.

After a long, involved religious ceremony (or, alternatively, a short strictly secular swap of I-dos,) the church or village bells chime and she proceeds, also preferably on foot, with her new husband to her family's home or to

The Wedding of Emma Bovary

True to her inner French girl, Emma Bovary had wanted a simple midnight wedding lit by torches, but she was forced to have a more traditional celebration. There were forty-three guests who remained sixteen hours at the table. Flaubert himself has said that the feast was "so grandiose that it had to be set up in a cart-shed, the only place on the grounds large enough to hold all the food and drink."

The table was laid under the cart-shed. On it were four sirloins, six chicken fricassees, stewed veal, three legs of mutton, and in the middle a fine roast suckling pig, flanked by four chitterlings with sorrel. At the corners were decanters of brandy. Sweet bottled-cider frothed round the corks, and all the glasses had been filled to the brim with wine beforehand. Large dishes of yellow cream, that trembled with the least shake of the table, had designed on their smooth surface the initials of the newly wedded pair in nonpareil arabesques. A confectioner of Yvetot had been entrusted with the tarts and sweets. As he had only just set up on the place, he had taken a lot of trouble, and at dessert he himself brought in a set dish that evoked loud cries of wonderment. To begin with, at its base there was a square of blue cardboard, representing a temple with porticoes, colonnades, and stucco statuettes all round, and in the niches constellations of gilt paper stars; then on the second stage was a dungeon of Savoy cake, surrounded by many fortifications in candied angelica, almonds, raisins, and quarters of oranges; and finally, on the upper platform a green field with rocks set in lakes of jam, nutshell boats,

Continued on next page . . .

and a small Cupid balancing himself in a chocolate swing whose two uprights ended in real roses for balls at the top.

Until night they ate. When any of them were too tired of sitting, they went out for a stroll in the yard, or for a game with corks in the granary, and then returned to table. Some towards the finish went to sleep and snored. But with the coffee everyone woke up. Then they began songs, showed off tricks, raised heavy weights, performed feats with their fingers, then tried lifting carts on their shoulders, made broad jokes, kissed the women. At night when they left, the horses, stuffed up to the nostrils with oats, could hardly be got into the shafts; they kicked, reared, the harness broke, their masters laughed or swore; and all night in the light of the moon along country roads there were runaway carts at full gallop plunging into the ditches, jumping over yard after yard of stones, clambering up the hills, with women leaning out from the tilt to catch hold of the reins.

Those who stayed at the Bertaux spent the night drinking in the kitchen. The children had fallen asleep under the seats.

an old, familiar restaurant, where the real celebration begins.

The food is delicious and copious. A sumptuous buffet of smoked salmon, caviar, *petits fours*, oysters, freshly baked breads, and enormous quantities of champagne. A dinner of four elaborate courses presented on a finely dressed table, followed by a giant pyramid of caramel-coated cream puffs called *croque-en-bouche* (crisp in the mouth). The wine flows from unlabeled bottles from the

Everything Wonderful About Weddings Is French

A little digging around in French history reveals that the French are the source of many of our own wedding customs.

The fanciful style of wedding gowns is attributed to Empress Eugénie, the bride of Napoleon III, and a major trend-setter in her time. White gowns became the custom after Anne of Brittany wore white when she married Louis XII in 1499.

The bride throws her garter thanks to a fourteenth-century bride who decided to toss her garter to guests for luck, rather than letting them tear bits of her dress, as had been the custom. Eventually another French bride threw her bouquet instead of her garter and the now traditional bouquet toss was born.

The *trousseau* (or "little bundle") originated in France. This bundle of clothing and linens a bride took with her to her new husband's home were collected and stored over the course of the French girl's life in a wedding armoire. This chest was built for her in her youth and given to the bridal couple as a gift from the bride's parents at the time of marriage.

Finally, the reception was born of an old French custom known as *charivari*, where friends and family of the bride and groom stood outside the newly marrieds' home, singing and clanging pots until invited in for refreshments. That's right, what we know as the reception used to be a prank.

local vineyard—or is exceptional vintage wine of the finest label.

There are flowers everywhere, laughter, abundant toasting and clinking of glasses. There is music—a local band playing favorite standards or a well-D.J.'ed collection of the bride and groom's favorite CDs. There is dancing, lots of dancing, especially for the French girl herself.

There is no time limit to the festivities. How can one put a cap on the genuine *joie de vivre* in attendance at the French girl's wedding? It may be the ultimate fête, for there is an exclusive *bonhomie* and a free-wheeling co-mingling of guests and flirtations that, heightened by the spirits of vintage wine, whet the general appetite for future couplings down the road.

Celebrations of the Season

Appropriately enough, one of the most "real" things about a French Christmas is food. In a country that does more with blood and brains than most Americans do with whole wheat and tomato, the French bring the whole farm to your foyer: With taxidermic flair butchers display large game birds, and whole pigs strangely festooned with herbs and ribbons, stretched out in mid-leap with their cloven hooves and snouts the size of softballs. In the less fleshy realm of food consumption, little French flags and roving musette bands herald the arrival of the latest Beaujolais nouveau. Boy Scouts sell homemade *tarte tatin* for

Le Film

COUSIN/COUSINE

The two weddings and various other celebrations in this 1975 movie are only slightly exaggerated versions of authentic French fêtes. The dancing, the drinking, the tangle of attractions and rejections. After you watch this, compare it to the Americanized film, called simply, *Cousins,* for a visual lesson in the difference between parties and *fêtes.*

five francs a slice. And chestnuts really *are* roasting on an open fire.

Those with family in the country leave Paris for little hamlets and snowy villages where people eat blood sausages and stuffed pheasant and drink enormous quantities of Bourgogne. My first French Christmas was spent in one such village, a place so deep in the heart of France that people actually start to resemble advertisements for packaged tours to the Dordogne. Against this backdrop for Rudolph's slope and sleigh there's little room for the mix-and-match, buffet-style religion that makes Americans seem like curious hybrids to the French. France is a largely Catholic, enthusiastically Christmas-celebrating country—and so far from my hometown that at one point between the *foie de veau* and the *poulet farci aux fines herbes*, a jovial in-law named Pierrot leaned over to me and asked with earnest curiosity if Americans celebrated Christmas.

Christmas is often a full-blown, full-color family (and community) affair for the French girl. The season usually begins on December 6th, the feast day of St. Nicholas. Some children receive candy treats and toys on this day from Père Noël, others find their shoes filled with gifts on Christmas morning. The French girl returns to her parents' or grandparents' home for the holiday, attending midnight service on Christmas Eve, followed by *le réveillon*, which means the awakening. Sidewalk cafes and restaurants are open all night for *le réveillon* while people feast on oysters, sausages, ham, roast fowl, fruit and pastries and wine. Enjoying *le réveillon* with family at home or surrounded by neighbors and friends at a local bistro— this is what many French girls are doing at 2:00 A.M. on Christmas morning.

Many of the accoutrements of the French girl's Christmas are familiar—though more refined and genuine than our own. A sprig of mistletoe over the door for good luck. A fir tree, decorated with fruits and candies, candles and stars, makes its appearance a few days—not a few weeks—before Christmas. The *crèche* or manger scene, which is found in nearly every church and many country homes, is made of glass or terra cotta or other simpler homemade materials.

For the French girl, there are authentic, meaningful symbols and traditions of the season, which is centered

Le Film

MA SAISON PRÉFÉRÉE
(My Favorite Season)

This film is about family and communication and the morphing of relationships over time. Catherine Deneuve is pitch perfect as Émilie, a lawyer and mother of limited emotional accessibility. Daniel Auteuil is also perfect as Antoine, her difficult, distanced brother. Émilie invites long estranged Antoine for Christmas Eve *réveillon*, which seemed to be going well enough until her husband, Bruno, and Antoine come to blows. It's good to know that holidays can be hell for families all over the globe, no?

around the family and extends from December 6th through January 6th (*not* five minutes after Halloween is over through the end of January sales). There is, of course, the traditional consumerism and advertising of the familiar Christmas nature; the department stores in Paris knock themselves out with elaborate lighting and extraordinary window displays of animated figures; confectioners' shops feature chocolate slopes-and-sleighs and buttery mocha Santas. But the holiday unfolds on a truer scale, with an emphasis on the experience rather than the trappings, on good food and wine over too many presents (and a credit hangover), on the family rather than the frenzy.

Bûche de Noël

If your inner French girl yearns for a taste of traditional Christmas in France and a holiday flight to Paris is out of the question, there's a delicious alternative. Make your own dessert masterpiece for dinner on Christmas Eve. A bûche de Noël is a decadent chocolate cake roll, covered in dark chocolate frosting to resemble bark and decorated with berries, holly, and meringue or marzipan mushrooms. Bûche de Noël means "yule log" in French, hearkening back to the old tradition of hauling huge logs from the woods to burn for twelve days, beginning on Christmas Eve. Perhaps if you eat bûche de Noël this Christmas, your luck will turn French. Look for these holiday cakes in most high quality bakeries in December, or try one of the many good recipes in cookbooks from Julia Child to *Joy of Cooking*.

Les Fêtes des Enfants

"What is a baby shower?" asked Nadine. "Do you actually put the baby in the shower or do you use the tub?" Thus began my conversation about baby showers with French girlfriend Nadine. How to explain the logic behind this American post-war boomer fête? We won the war, we were celebrating the goodwill of convenient new technologies, like plastic, and we were busy making lots of ba-

Père Noël vs. Santy Claus

Of so many differences between French and American Christmas perhaps the most delicious is the difference between the antique and authentic Père Noël (Father Christmas) and our own corporate-sponsored Mr. Claus. Here are the highlights:

FRENCH PÈRE NOËL

Père Noël has been giving gifts for so long in Europe that he's become a spartan soul. Little Claudette might get one wooden block set and a small doll for Christmas. *Pas plus!*

Cookies and milk by the fireplace are entirely unacceptable. Père Noël expects leftovers from an eight-course meal and a small shot glass of cognac. Like all French saints he's concerned about his liver but, what the hell, you only live once.

Père Noël works with a partner and it isn't the little missus. It's Père Fouettard, a humorless bloke whose job it is to remind Père Noël of how each child has behaved during the past year. The little French girl fears Père Fouettard, no doubt because according to folklore, he sports a whip. ("Fouet" means "whip" in French)

Père Noël loathes publicity and will not show his face until early December. The little French girl waits impatiently for his arrival.

Continued on next page . . .

AMERICAN SANTA CLAUS

Santa's got a new low-APR credit card with unlimited credit and so many gifts to deliver that his sleigh won't do. He's got a new four-wheel steel-enhanced sports utility sled that gets about three miles to the gallon.

Santa has unionized elves who come along for the ride to watch a digitized version of *Frosty the Snowman* on the backseat VCR. (His reindeer were "liberated" by animal rights protestors years ago.)

Santa is concerned about his cholesterol and the many pounds he's put on over the last century. He'll drink the milk if it's nonfat and eat the cookies if they're Snackwell's.

Santa's got a new PR director whose mission is to get his face in front of American children *before* Halloween. The little American girl pretends she believes in Santa Claus so her parents will give her that remote control Barbie-on-the-Riviera cigarette boat.

bies—hence the need for lots of baby things. Meanwhile, France was digging itself out of the rubble and still dealing with the problematic realities of a nineteenth-century existence, baby making among them.

"Why celebrate the arrival of a baby who has not yet arrived?" Nadine persisted. "Does that not bring very bad luck?" The ghosts of history and a predilection for avoiding anything themed has kept the baby shower resolutely off the French girl's radar screen.

American culture has become so child-centric it's hard to imagine the little French girl's birthday party. No purple dinosaur entertainment, no fifteen-foot moon bouncer. No cake the size of a carport. Just a simple little get-together of a tiny handful of children, one or two nice but not elaborate gifts, and an honest homemade cake. The birthday girl feels special but not unduly lavished upon and life goes on as ever on a reasonable, even keel.

There might be a little family clink of glasses when the French girl passes her *baccalauréat* exam. The *bac* is a nationwide exam that, when successfully passed, is the equivalent of our high-school diploma and all roads and studies lead to the *bac*. If she passes (which is not easy) she has an important credential that enables her path in a career or higher education. Her parents are flush with pride, and the French girl is on her way!

Between bourgeois Paris (Left Bank) and working-class Paris (Right Bank)—on the other side of the tracks, across

Borrow a Page from the French Girl's Book: Tradition and Celebration

Spend time, not money, on holiday traditions. As with all things French girl, less is more. Cook, eat, drink, and gather to create memories and community. Create rituals of celebration. Pass them on.

A French Halloween

Every Halloween the French ask how a pagan holiday of Celtic origin became an American phenomenon—and a $14-billion-a-year-business. So perhaps out of sheer consternation (or perhaps so merchants can generate more foot traffic by selling pumpkin-shaped madeleines), the French have begun to reclaim the fête, but with some Gaelic modifications. When a group of French neighbors teamed up to spread the Halloween ritual in our neighborhood, the results were, well, different.

Trick or treating through Parisian apartment buildings has its inherent limitations—there are security codes to know, intercoms to buzz. And the French, who don't open their doors easily to *n'importe qui*, were perplexed by the idea that a raggedy band of children would come marching to their doorstep, demanding candy no less. Signs had been posted at elevators and ground floor entrances explaining that a group of ghouls and goblins would be arriving on the 31st in need of some *bonbons*; still, many French folks just didn't get it. ("Mardi gras is Brazilian, no?" asked one elderly gentleman.)

There were a few strawberry and honey bee toddlers, and the requisite Batmen in loose tights and parkas (it was cold that Halloween, bitterly cold), but overall the French trick-or-treaters were dressed in individual, stylized fashion: There was a half-pirate half-cyclops, a gypsy dancer, a spy in black leotards and red beret, a papier-mâché pig. Just saying "trick or treat" (which has no meaningful equivalent in French, beyond "*farce ou friandise*") was unacceptable (too curt, not polite in view of the candy), so one neighbor came up with a complex opera riff involving a round that the kids sang over the course

Continued on next page . . .

of three long minutes, all of them eager to get to the candy but well-behaved enough to wait and not pounce once the well-intentioned neighbor judiciously parceled out the candy one by one (". . . and here is one *bonbon* for Jacques, and one *bonbon* for Marie-Nadine, and one *bonbon* for Pierre . . ."). The children were instructed that the candy was to be eaten over the course of the remaining year—something they all seemed to accept without so much as a whimper.

A light rain began to fall on bat ears and berets as the *troupe* made its way to another neighbor's house, where the novelty of a pumpkin pie was waiting. Pumpkin is not a familiar ingredient to the French. In this case, our neighbor had bought a fresh pumpkin, scooped out the skin and made a genuine, fresh pumpkin pie using crème fraîche, freshly grated nutmeg, cracked cloves and rum. It took a bit of encouragement to convince several youngsters to try the pie— "I can't eat any pie that's made from a vegetable," one Batman declared—but once they did, a good time was had by all.

the Seine, in the urban density of the city's northern fringe, a different kind of party takes place in a different kind of Paris. This is where Edith Piaf grew up, where ragamuffins and hooligans once reigned; where Truffaut and others shot glorious black-and-white footage of the rough edges of town. Quarry pits and windmills once rose high above the city here, and people came to drink *guinguet* (cheap wine) and dance. Today, it's a portal for immigrants arriving in France. It is polyglot, multi-cultural, post-colonial. Artists have refurbished old bakeries and created vast airy lofts where, once a year, they open their doors in a famous city art walk. They share walls with families from China, North Africa and Central Europe. This is Paris of contortionists and accordionists, of philosophers and thespians, of working class merchants and bohemian aristocrats. This is People's Paris.

Perhaps in an effort to inspire unity in this rapidly changing landscape, perhaps just for the hell of it, City Hall had decided to launch an annual street party—"block party" in American terms. Never mind that there is no such thing as a block party in France. Or that the French don't co-mingle with strangers for anything other than a concert or a political protest. Or even that they might adore their *arrondissement*, but they don't particularly care to meet their neighbors and they don't do potlucks. "I'd only go to a 'block party' to pick up a nice woman," one friend sniffed in a condescending manner. Still, like many others, he came. And he conquered.

Forget the six-packs. Forget the plastic cutlery and paper plates. Forget the economy-size bags of chips. A French block party might be a curiosity but it's no less French. People ambled into the courtyard of a building in front of the main church with their own china and porcelain wrapped in thin blankets and stashed in baskets, along with an array of perfectly prepared food. In fact it was the food and drink that broke the ice—the berry pies dusted with powdered sugar. The piping hot spinach and chèvre quiche with doughy homemade crust. The couscous and grilled lamb with mint leaves and saffron rice. The Chinese dumplings and honey almond cakes. The grilled tomatoes and fist-sized mushrooms. And the vast quantities of wine (Saint Émillion, Pomerol, Côtes du Rhône, Pauillac). This slightly fractious, tentative group of multicultural strangers eventually did forge a certain unity. In the staid formality of Paris, where districts segment the city like so many slices of perfectly cut Brie, here was an unusual opportunity for the conservative working-class butcher to party with his African neighbor; for the slightly stuffy school administrator to knock back a brandy with the Vietnamese shopkeeper; for the busy executive who shuttles to La Défense every day to loosen his tie and co-mingle with a Moroccan drummaker or a Tunisian mechanic. This was Paris in the new millennium, the new French melting pot. A lanky young man took out an accordion and played muzette. Someone dragged a piano against an open window and began playing Chopin. Another neighbor who was a permanent fixture at the *pharmacie* began to sing opera (to everyone's astonishment), while a couple of rangy cats sampled the *foie gras*.

The talk was decidedly civic at first and went on for hours. ("When are we going to get the dog problem under control in this neighborhood? Have you seen the exhibit at the new music museum near La Villette? What about our bumbling mayor? Did you hear that the rue de Meaux will soon be pedestrian-only?") But eventually couples formed, phone numbers were scribbled on the back of metro stubs, the public persona gave way to a more private face.

By evening those with families had retired for the night, but the younger crowd kept on in raucous after-hour partying. No one, of course, called the cops. You never do, anyhow, in Paris, no matter how loud a late-night party gets. Everyone is complicit in the act of partying in Paris, even if it means tolerating the right of others to prevent you from sleeping. In this instance, however, the people could now place a name with the (loud) face making noise outside, and this made the ruckus all the more acceptable. If this hadn't been the motive of City Hall to begin with, it certainly was now.

Fin

In many ways, the French are true party animals. There need not be any logical reason to celebrate—to clink glasses in a simple fête or throw together a dinner party. When my husband works on a film shoot, the French crew systematically throws a cocktail party at the end of every work week—no matter how late (and it's often extremely late), no matter how exhausted the crew might be (and they're always exhausted), no matter where they might be (Africa, Iceland, it doesn't matter). Perhaps it's the fact that life can be both good and bad, has its ups and downs, its highs and lows—and that each upswing must be celebrated. Perhaps it's just for the hell of it—a natural hu-

man inclination that, as Nadine once put it, keeps us just
a little bit more civilized than, say, the orangutan. Whatever the case may be, the party—or *la fête*—is one of
those deeply rooted "fundamental things" that Wharton
reminds us to consider in her analysis of the French *style
de vie*. Celebrate life, the French girl might implore us, or
it will pass you by.

Six

La Maison

To get to Karine's home in Paris you take the metro to the Bastille stop. You go up the old cobblestones of the trendy rue de Lappe, past the rocking Club Le Balajo and down a tiny somewhat forlorn-looking street (unnamed), where you'll find a little red door in a once opulent, now decrepit old mansion from the seventeenth century. You ring the

"It's not houses I love, it's the life I live in them."
COCO CHANEL

buzzer and hope Karine will hear you. If she does, she'll buzz open the door, and you'll walk up seven winding, creaking flights (the elevator's been broken for five years). At the end of the dark hallway, you'll see Karine's door, which will be ajar. Once inside, you will be surprised to step in and discover a wide open, glorious little space where the best of the Old and the New World have come together. Exposed wooden beams on the ceiling and original parquet floors, with large windows that let in the stunning white light of the Parisian sky. The furniture is both mod and cozy, elegant and funky. There are few things here, but each piece has a personality of its own: A large piece of original artwork hung, ceremoniously and with singular precision, above an authentic oak chair. A well-worn Persian carpet and a kitschy lamp from the 1950s. You immediately want to sit down and read. Or cross your legs and cogitate. Or knock back a whisky and dance. There's something in the space—call it soul, call it energy—that is so clearly a reflection of the inhabitant's aesthetic. And I've experienced this sense of place in the home of every French girl I know.

Writing in the mid-1900s, French philosopher Gaston Bachelard defined home as "our corner of the world. It is our first universe, a real cosmos in every sense of the word. If we look at it intimately, the humblest dwelling has beauty."

The French girl's "corner of the world" is warm and usually smaller than its American counterpart. It is intimate by default, by architecture, by design, by historical imperative. So much lived experience is jumbled into small spaces in her world, so much busy layering and patterning of life, that while she may renovate or redecorate, her home always becomes more of who she is over time. And the sense of time—the feeling that a space has been truly lived-in—is another element that is inextricably linked to the French home and its charm. "I have never been on stairs that don't creak," one French girlfriend said in awe as she walked up the large, pristine staircase in an American house while vacationing in the States. "It just doesn't feel natural. It is a queer sensation. Here is a house that does not speak!"

Equally part and parcel of the French home is its sense of permanence. Because the French have a deeply-rooted sense of place, they don't move as frequently as Americans (in fact, they relocate less frequently than any other Europeans). They don't demolish and reconstruct. To maintain the historical and aesthetic integrity of buildings, they respect a mandate to keep façades intact while renovating interiors. They ask themselves how an old space can be modified, how its original soul can linger. In this fashion, houses and homes have a certain immutability about them, and often boundless charm.

Within these homes, the French girl often avoids the showy accumulation of things for the sake of things. There is a tendency in French life to exude a certain tasteful frugality no matter what one's social standing. So it is often the French girl of noble background who rides a rusty bicycle to her open market in the French countryside, wearing an old sweater with tattered but lovely hems, and whose country home has the elegant, disheveled air of a woman who has more important things to do than worry about appearances or impressing people. And in fact, her desire not to impress is impressive in and of itself.

If the French girl is lucky enough to live in an eighteenth- or nineteenth-century apartment, the sheer architectural splendor of the building itself (the marble chimney, the vaulted ceilings, the softly worn parquet wood floors) assumes a life of its own, and the ghosts of the past will imbue her home with lingering character. Says a French girlfriend of her home: "This apartment has been in my family for generations. My grandmother was born here. My mother. And of course so was I. We've changed the furniture and artwork to suit our tastes but it will always have a certain aura of its own."

French Girl Style

The French aesthetic is not one thing—it's many things, layered, textured and idiosyncratic. But you'll invariably stumble upon four variations on the theme once French

The Doorknob

"When I move into a new apartment, which I don't do very often, I want to have the feeling that I will live there the rest of my life. So I take great pains to make it the perfect space. I don't shortcut anything." So began a lengthy discussion with Chantale about, among other things, her pursuit of the perfect doorknob. Chantale had recently bought an apartment on the rue de Seine after living nearly twenty years on the rue St. Dominque (two streets that no one, in their right mind, would ever want to leave). For her new apartment, she became obsessed with finding the perfect doorknob for each room. Here is a very busy woman (Chantale works at one of the busiest French newspapers), but she managed to invest serious time and patience in her quest for everything from drawer handles to ceiling moldings. She criss-crossed the center of Paris, her dissatisfaction driving her off the beaten path, into unknown *arrondissements* at the edge of the city limits. She finally found one perfect doorknob for her bathroom—"it is made of beautiful glass, just the right shade of grey-blue, the perfect size for the hand, very 'graspable' and lovely . . ."—in a tiny ramshackle hardware store in a working-class part of town. She also ended up buying the perfect mixing bowl here, simple lucite shower rings ("not too small, but not too big, either"), a set of wooden mixing spoons, a bright yellow butter dish and three extra perfect doorknobs, "just in case." Her quest for other perfect doorknobs continues.

French Girls We Love

PAULINE DE ROTHSCHILD

For her creativity and skill in turning every home into a fairy-tale work of striking elegance. Even before marrying Baron Philippe de Rothschild in 1954, she used her unerring eye and sense of beauty to make a two-room apartment a stunning showpiece. For example, her drawing room, while modestly proportioned, was done in all white, with simple silk curtains, two Louis XVI pieces, and incredible floral arrangements. The pièce de résistance: real gold leaf moldings. Once she had the resources of unlimited wealth at her disposal, she went to work on decorating her Paris flat, a separate house Philippe lived in, and the Château Mouton, a Gothic relic at the vineyard her husband owned. Her aesthetic is described in *The Power of Style* this way: "Her objects were of such beauty, such quality, and so artfully placed, it seemed as if she were not decorating with but rather paying homage to them. Her philosophy was that if there was nothing fine enough to fill the space, leave it bare." Yet she also believed in the practical; thus, her famous French blue library was filled not only with an extensive collection of books, it had pullout tables, chairs, lamps, pads and pencils beneath every shelf. In typical

Continued on next page

girls open their private doors to you: Classic, Chic, Bohemian, and Provincial.

The *classic* look takes its cues from the courtly Rococo opulence of Louis XV and the late Middle Ages. This aristocratic aesthetic, with its somewhat predictable affec-

Rothschild fashion, however, Pauline added turquoise velvet sofas.

To run multiple households as gracefully as she did, Baroness de Rothschild applied extraordinary organizational ability. Each morning, she'd browse through huge books of fabric swatches and photos of her china, silver, tablecloths, and napkins. From nearly two hundred patterns, she'd choose the items to design stunning table landscapes for her nightly guests, adding natural elements such as ferns, mosses, cherry branches, or ornamental kale. Her attention to detail, together with her vision and exquisite taste, meant every house she adorned became a castle. Read *The Power of Style* by Annette Tapert and Diana Edkins.

tions, usually features stately Baroque furniture, heavy oriental rugs, Lalique vases, gigantic seventeenth- or eighteenth-century wall tapestries, busts of historical figures, and plenty of dark wood paneling. These homes, often reflecting the tastes of the reigning (and somewhat waning) nobility, evoke a certain nostalgia for the storybook, colonial France of days long gone.

The *chic* home reflects just the opposite: Usually sparse and Zenlike, the chic French home is sophisticated, ultramodern and oriented entirely toward the future. This home revolves around a few well-chosen, high-end designer pieces, often with a color scheme of black on white or similar simple contrasts. Where the walls of the classic home might be covered in busy, tightly-illustrated floral wallpaper, the chic home is industrial bare, with a stylish absence of visual noise. You must be educated in the fine art of art itself to discern in the rarified simplicity of the truly chic home the personal quirks and passions of the French girl who lives here.

The *bohemian* look is *all* about personal quirks and passions. This is where French funk reigns and rules are decidedly not followed. You're likely to see a Tunisian parchment lamp next to a Louis-Philippe-style chair in this home. Things are acquired with the collector's eye in flea markets and through travels. The preference here is for the mismatched, the handmade, and the vintage, and the overall look is often indefinably eclectic and arty.

The *provincial* home rings a more folksy note, with a singular preference for authentic, natural materials. Baskets, ceramic pottery, multi-colored glass jars, authentically aged wooden tables and unfinished chairs, big bouquets of dried flowers—the provincial home has a thoroughly cozy, rural appeal. Where the classic home will be set with the opulent precision of a stage set, the provincial home exudes a comfortable nonchalance and is frayed at the edges, weathered by the elements. Where the chic or bohemian home may have a coded aesthetic, with artistic persuasions that are very personal, the provincial home is entirely down-home: This is where you eat freshly baked bread and local goat cheese with your elbows on the table and the kitchen door flung wide open.

House and Home

"What's going on here?" Corinne asked as we drove through the suburbs of upscale Los Angeles for the first time. "These houses are all confused. They are having an identity crisis!" Corinne was referring to the heterogeneity of the architecture. For her, a real house must be at least one hundred years old and be quarried from the same stone as other houses in the community. A real house does not have Greek arches, Spanish tile, Tudor-style windows, a Roman portico and a ranch-style backyard—all in the same floor plan. It is unified. It has a certain permanence to it. It has a man-sized fireplace reminiscent of hearth and home cooking, not a blue flame of gas and fake brick. It has creaky stairs and imposing masonry. It is what it is: a house, not a theme park, not a showcase for different styles.

After a few hours in Los Angeles, however, Corinne softened up to what she call the "nouvelle California-style eclecticism." She realized that compared to the urban history of Paris or Lyon, Los Angeles is not even on the map. "Then again, there is a certain exuberance in all this diversity, I guess," she conceded, reconsidering her judgments as we passed a twenty-foot donut. "I guess you Americans can get away with shameless bad taste. Eventually, something good could become of it."

Le Film

BLUE

This is one third of Krzysztof Kieslowski's trilogy of *Red, White,* and *Blue*. It stars Juliette Binoche as Julie, a moody French girl in this classically moody French film. Kieslowski uses color (blue, of course) and off camera angles and flashbacks and music (which is almost a character in the story)—all the great tricks in a French filmmaker's bag. And the film also features three homes—Julie's country home, her bohemian apartment in Paris, and her friend's stylish and sophisticated bachelor pad. See this movie to get an eyeful of French home style. And see it to observe a French girl stripped of everything but the very ordinary clothes on her back and an excellent haircut—and still looking smart and stylish and ever so French.

To Tour the French Girl's Home

The French are often surprised by the American tendency to give first-time guests a full tour of their home before even popping the cork over drinks. While being invited into the French girl's home is a true sign that a personal frontier has been crossed, there are still boundaries to respect, and the French girl will rarely give a full tour of each room in her home until she knows you well.

Le Livre

ELLE DÉCOR: THE GRAND BOOK OF
FRENCH STYLE
by François Baudot and Jean Demachy

This book, by the editors of the French magazine, covers interiors from Provence, chalet, and country, to eclectic, eccentric and classic chic. Modern French designers—think Philippe Starck and Yves Saint Laurent—are explored along with gorgeous "real-life" homes. If you're not inspired to decorate like a French girl, you can leave it on your coffee table and pretend.

Le Foyer

The French girl's foyer is the literal portal to her world. It's a practical threshold: an umbrella and coat stand accommodate the tangle of coats and hats. A mirror lets everyone gather their wits—to smooth wind-tussled hair or straighten an upturned collar. But the foyer is only the spatial preamble to the central heart of her home—the living room, or *le salon*.

Le Salon

It was a French noblewoman named Catherine de Rambouillet who, bored with predictable seventeenth-century courtly life, sought out thinkers, intellectuals and philosophers to animate the dreary opulence of her aristocratic life. Rambouillet transformed her living room into an intellectual power place, a room where the fine art of conversation could reign. Thus, the salon was born.

The salon remains to this day the central hub and soul of French life. Since many French apartments don't have separate dining rooms (and their kitchens are impossibly small), the salon has a preeminently practical and multifunctional role in the French girl's life. It's where she loves to lounge in blissful solitude and also where she entertains groups of people—and she often configures things with both functions in mind. Her couch and chairs are arranged in a comfortable U-shape, close to one another (never at an icy distance), so guests naturally face one another rather than stare off into space or, worse, toward a TV or "entertainment center." Where electronica reigns in many traditional American living rooms, books are king in the French one, and they're present everywhere: lined up in built-in bookshelves, spilling onto the floor in small piles with well-worn spines and dog-eared pages.

A low table is a prerequisite in the French girl's home, and it's often set between couch and chairs to accommodate a cocktail spread. A separate table is set up in a different part of the living room with dining accoutrements and often an opulent vase of flowers. Thus the salon/dining room occupy one space. When the salon is too small to configure two separate spaces, everything takes place at the table—which is usually set back against a wall during the day. When the French girl has the good fortune

French Girls We Love

MADAME CATHERINE DE RAMBOUILLET

For being so original and sophisticated—and not only by seventeenth-century standards. She designed her home in Paris herself, one of the first to use the color blue for a main room, as opposed to the customary red or cream. Beginning around 1610, after marrying the Marquis de Rambouillet, she would invite guests to a weekly salon of conversation and gossip. Another of her innovations was moving the main staircase to the side in order to have all the salon rooms open on to each other.

to have a separate dining room, it's often an extension of the living room in taste and décor.

These limitations of space reinforce a general intimacy in French life, and the insatiable American drive for space is foreign and sometimes comical to the French. "Eventually, you Americans will have a separate room for every person, including a special bathroom for each pet, and your rooms will be so large you will be able to avoid authentic human contact at all costs!" Chantale opined over a glass of wine one night. I'm sure it was the wine talking.

The salon is the public face of the private French girl. Along with her books her home is a gallery of curios, found objects, heirlooms, paintings, photographs, musical instruments. She'll usually have an old buffet where she stores good china and wine glasses, and a stash of

Where Her Home Furnishings Come From

Habitat and Conran Shop for modern furniture that lasts. Ikea for simple basics. Le Monde Sauvage for high-end ethnic-style furniture. Capellini for top-of-the-line Italian designers. Bensimon for high-design home accessories and simple clothes. Muji for must-have Japanese stationery, office supplies and simple clothes; Ordning & Reda for cool edible-looking Swedish stationery; Caligrane for luxurious stationery. Monoprix for dishes, little appliances, and practical things (bowls, soap dishes, organizers) and hair accessories. All the other countless boutiques for unique finds and one-of-a-kind bric-a-brac. Ditto for flea markets.

excellent liqueur. She often prefers standing lamps over traditional overhead lighting for the intimate glow and warm mood. The French girl will also create cozy nooks in her salon: an ottoman propped against an empty wall; a small cluster of chairs around a reading table.

Le Boudoir

For centuries the bedroom was a public space where births, deaths and even political meetings took place. (Louis XIV was partial to the latter.) The French revolution, with a little help from Madame de Pompadour, changed all that.

Les Lumières

Firelight, lamp light, candle light, moody light. Things that glow, flicker, twinkle, incandesce . . . Lighting is a crucial element in the French girl's home. She plays with light as an accent, an enhancer and in ways that are rarely strictly functional. Nothing, for example, is nicer than kind, romantic lighting at a party. Even the glorious Catherine Deneuve knows how to play with shadows and light. When she walks into a room, she'll draw a curtain away from an unflattering glare—after forty years in the film business, she knows a thing or two about casting a good light.

Today, while we have an incredible array of beds thanks to the French, the contemporary French bedroom is unequivocally private. This is the French girl's intimate habitat. It's her place for reading, making love, eating breakfast in bed. It's where she thinks, broods, dreams, and schemes. She often has a stately armoire (remember, good closet space is not French) for all her clothes and a few of the same sorts of well-chosen personal objects that occupy the rest of her home. Her books are often stacked high on her bedside table in an intriguing literary jumble.

The French girl usually prefers warm colors in her bedroom. This is where her walls might be warm red velvet or savory chocolate brown and her lighting enhances the room with a muted interplay of shadow and light.

If there's any *pièce de résistance* in her bedroom it's her bed, where history has slipped into her sheets. Her bed is often made "the French way": The head of her bed is graced by a long thin bolster-type pillow called a *traversin* which is sometimes removed at night. Big square pillows in pure cotton shams are propped up against the *traversin*. Most French girls have gone Scandinavian with duvets (one for summer, one for winter) though some still prefer the traditional sheet and blanket approach. If her bed is on a frame, a bed skirt is used not only to decorate, but also to conceal extra linens that the closet-deprived French girl might store underneath.

Like everything else in her life her bed has its secrets. Its stories to tell. It is both practical and sensual, dedicated entirely to pleasure.

French Girls We Love
COLETTE

For making her Parisian flat in the Palais Royal so appealing to her sensual nature when she was forced by illness to take to her bed for the last decade of her life. Special Colette touches were to wallpaper the ceiling to avoid any blank white space; pushing her divan, which she dubbed her "raft," close enough to the window to watch the changing scene; and putting a blue bulb in a lamp shaded with her signature blue writing paper. A large collection of crystal paperweights, her own needlework on the chairs, and an antique writing desk she retrofitted with wheels added to the room's charm. Red was Colette's favorite color, and red paper covered the walls, also hung with her mounted butterflies. Chocolates, bowls of fruit, plenty of flowers in various vases, perfume-filled air, and fur pelisses on her lap made chez Colette très Colette. Read Colette's *Cheri*, *Break of Day*, and *Gigi*, for starters. And read *Earthly Paradise: Colette's Autobiography Drawn from her Lifetime Writings* by Robert Phelps, an assemblage of passages from her books and letters that paints a vivid picture of her life.

La Salle de Bain

The French girl exercises the same discretion in this private boudoir as she does in the rest of her home. While she might keep her cosmetic clutter out of sight, hidden in beautiful boxes or colorful cases, she'll display other

French Girls We Love

JOSEPHINE BONAPARTE

For setting Napoleon's "blood on fire." And for her enviable social skills and characteristic good taste, both of which were instrumental to Napoleon as he tried to build a respectable imperial court. Château de Malmaison, the home Bonaparte built for Josephine as a refuge from court life on the outskirts of Paris, was furnished by Charles Percier and Pierre François Léonard Fontaine, Napoleon's architects, originators of the "Empire" style and the most important decorators in France. Josephine's boudoir was fitted with bronze tables, fabric-covered walls and a *lit de repos* (day bed) draped with curtains suspended from a round canopy. After the inevitable divorce from Bonaparte because she had not borne an heir, Josephine moved permanently to Château de Malmaison, where she remained a friend to Napoleon and continued to give extravagant parties on the allowance he provided (though in his letters he discouraged her spending). She loved to garden and spent her retirement growing and tending to rare and exotic plants. Read Sandra Gulland's three-volume fictionalized biography, *The Many Lives and Secret Loves of Josephine B.*, *Tales of Passion, Tales of Woe* and *The Last Great Dance on Earth*, all of which read like Josephine's personal diaries. For a nonfiction account of Josephine's relationship with Bonaparte, read *Napoleon & Josephine: An Improbable Marriage* by Evangeline Bruce.

utilitarian objects with an almost curatorial flourish: big fragrant bars of milled, flamboyantly embossed soaps, beautiful bottles of aromatic oil, an ancient Japanese comb or a collection of river stones. The French girl usu-

Clutter

Marguerite Duras, for all of her unconventional and libertine ways, had an old fashioned love of home. She had curious and emphatic opinions on matters ranging from men and children in the home to which basic supplies no well-run home should be without. She had a particular position on the subject of clutter and disorder in a home. "Some women can never manage it—they can't handle their houses, they overload them, clutter them up, never create an opening towards the world outside . . . [There is] outer and inner order in a house. The outer order is the visible running of the house, and the inner order is that of the ideas, emotional phases, and endless feelings" associated with its inhabitants.

To Duras there was charm and there was clutter. Charm represented the little details that reflected the character of the people who lived in a home. These are the accents and appointments that make home a place not to leave, but to stay with through the ages. Clutter, on the other hand, is a helpless, hopeless, giving over to disorder and, according to Duras, makes a house unbearable so that family leaves as soon as they can get a ticket out of town. The trick is to see the difference between charm and clutter: Charm reflects your history, your affinities, your essence; clutter does not.

ally has a simple rug to take the chill off a cold bathroom floor and a single flower set off against a frieze of tiles.

Beyond its obvious practical functions, the French girl's bathroom might be playful. The French are notorious for their ribald sense of humor (think of Rabelais, who was

so ribald he enjoys his own adjective), and they sometimes let more than their hair down in bathrooms. Wild
artwork and slightly salacious reading are sometimes
found in the French bathroom. In one chic Parisian café,
each bathroom stall has a peep hole that promises a
sneaky private view into the adjacent stall, but in fact
looks onto a tiny diorama of city life. The French bathroom has a certain elegant grace, but it also knows how
to take a joke.

La Cuisine

Serendipity (she was my neighbor) and a natural curiosity
about one another (I was the foreign American, she was
the original French girl) led me with enthusiastic regularity into Martine's kitchen, where she would conjure up
extraordinary hungry-man meals with enviable nonchalance. Like most French girls' kitchens, Martine's was tiny

Aromatherapy at Home

The scent-conscious French girl has an apothecary filled with different aromas for different rooms. Potpourri or pomanders may line her dresser drawers; perfumed pillows or sachets might be tucked into sofa corners; fragrant candles are placed on side tables. In her bedroom she might diffuse the sultry scents of rose, ylang ylang, nutmeg or clary sage. Or release the cleansing, citrus scents of lemon, grapefruit, and bergamot in her bathroom. French girl uses aromatherapy to create a mood, to heal, and to set off a particular aromatic ambiance. Volumes have been written on the subject. She owns at least one of them.

and compact, but she made the most of it. She was not preoccupied with stainless steel or colossal ranges (hers was a modest four-burner gas stove). Her refrigerator was small, and she liked it that way. It forced her to do smaller and more frequent shoppings of fresher, choicer fare. Many of her cooking wares were exposed: big cast-iron and copper pots, large wooden spoons and soup ladles in oversized pitchers, dried herbs in glass bottles on open shelves along with exotic tea tins; big slabs of creamy cheese set out to ripen. Her kitchen was a colorful and sometimes mysterious epicurean jumble but she always had just what she needed (no more, no less) to make exactly what she desired (no more, no less) for however

Le Livre

THE FRAGRANT YEAR
by Claire Louise Hunt

This book focuses on the use of scent in the home, with an emphasis on seasonal colors and scents. It's inspirational and practical—and a good place to start thinking about scent as accent in your home.

many people she wanted to feed. I would often sit on the edge of a wooden stool and watch her cook, tending to the machinations of meal-making, and thank my lucky stars for good French neighbors and their small, brilliantly creative little kitchens.

Other Corners of the French Girl's Home

A well-filled attic is the sign of a well-lived life, and the French girl invariably has a country home where the benevolent ghosts of the past live in "*le grenier*": A rusty rocking horse permanently frozen in half-gallop; boxes of outgrown clothes with broken hems and missing buttons; books read under a blooming linden tree one distant summer long ago. This storybook space is not relentlessly organized and swept clean but left to accumulate the poetic fragments of the past; a small alcove where her children can rummage and ramble; a place of continuity and gentle clutter, where a small object and can set off, like

La Liste

Marguerite Duras, a very serious homemaker in the classic sense of the word, kept a list of the things that should always be in a house on the wall of the kitchen in her country home at Neauphle-le-Château.

table salt	butter	lavatory paper
pepper	tea	light bulbs
sugar	flour	kitchen soap
coffee	eggs	Scotchbrite
wine	tinned tomatoes	eau de Javel (bleach)
potatoes	kitchen salt	washing powder (hand)
pasta	Nescafé	Spontex
rice	nuoc mam	Ajax
oil	bread	steel wool
vinegar	cheeses	coffee filters
onions	yogurt	fuses
garlic	window cleaner	insulating tape
milk		

Said Duras of the list:

"The list is still there, on the wall. We haven't added anything. We haven't taken to using any of the hundreds of new articles that have been invented in the twenty years since it was written."

Le Livre

A WELL KEPT HOME: HOUSEHOLD TRADITIONS
AND SIMPLE SECRETS FROM A FRENCH
GRANDMOTHER
by Laura Fronly and Yves Duronson

Just opening this book causes you to slow down and smell
the French roses. The author collects home and kitchen and
garden rituals and tips and solutions that she learned from
her French grandmother. The book is loaded with terrific in-
formation, but never lets us forget the pleasure of simple
things done well—the French way.

snow in a glass globe, a flurry of drifting memories. "The mind sees and continues to see objects," wrote Bachelard, "while the spirit finds the nest of immensity in an object."

The French girl's home also contains boxes and chests that vary in function and form, from an antique little box that holds buttons to an old-fashioned valise that peeks out from under her bed and contains winter woolens. At the end of each season, she has her ritual: She repacks these boxes and valises with clothes that are either too heavy or too light, and replaces them with clothes for the next season. Space being at a premium, her closets aren't teeming with things that need to be posted and hauled off to the Salvation Army. There is order and purpose to these places: not an inch is not artfully, but practically considered.

PRACTICALITIES
by Marguerite Duras

While she says in the opening pages that she "doesn't have general views about anything except social injustice," internationally acclaimed author Marguerite Duras gets as personal as any self-respecting French girl can get in these brief spoken essays on everything from shopping lists and housework to men ("You have to be very fond of [men] to love them. Otherwise they're simply unbearable.") Many of the people, scenes and places mentioned in this book are the inspirations for her works. Read *Practicalities*, written with the help of interviewer Jérôme Beaujour and published in English in 1990, to appreciate Duras's novels even more.

Fin

I once took a French girlfriend out to Malibu. Along the way she looked up at a community of trailer homes parked high on a craggy hill and asked, "What's that?" I tried to explain the concept of trailer homes ("You know, houses on wheels? Like, really, really huge Winnebagos that you live in but don't drive?") but she didn't seem to understand. "This cannot be a house if it is meant to move," she said, ignoring the fact that the trailer homes hadn't actually moved in several decades. ("So, if they haven't moved," she persisted, "why do you call them

Borrow A Page from the French Girl's Book: Home

Forge a home according to your own unique tastes. Take the time to accumulate meaningful objects. Let history into your home. Create comfortable spaces for wining, dining and conversing. Invest in an excellent dining table that seats at least six. Light your space well, but gently. See your own unique, distinct signature in every room in your home. Be picky. Go off the beaten path for doorknobs and details. Live in your home like you'll be there the rest of your life.

trailer homes?") The concept of a house that moves is so antithetical to what a house is all about, that the French girl can barely embrace the notion. She and her compatriots move less than their European neighbors, and even the mere thought of relocating fills her with a particular dread. Her home is a bastion of personal and family history. It's her inner world made manifest, where her sensual passions and her practical nature converge. No matter how much I tried, my French friend could not accept that anything without a sense of permanence and a sense of place could be considered a true home. If home is where the heart is (so the logic goes), then the heart must be firmly planted in order to grow.

Le Travail et Le Loisir

When you do business in France, leave your time management seminars, your One-Minute Managers, your productivity workshops and your ideas about dressing for success behind. Keep your down-home Protestant work ethic if you like, but don't expect anyone else to be pulling all-nighters or admiring your multi-tasking skills. Think about pursuing that midlife career change, but keep it to yourself. And if you want a successful business lunch, put aside at least two hours for schmoozing over wine, several courses, and dessert.

French life revolves more around security and leisure than the pursuit of the Next Big Thing—be it a new career or a new entrepreneurial endeavor. The government supports a system that gives workers an enviable amount of job security, generously subsidizes cultural pursuits, pays its intellectuals to be, well, intellectual, and grants its citizens a luxurious number of paid vacation days. All of which means that when push comes to shove in the world of work and play, we Anglo-Saxons might know how to make a living, but the French girl knows how to have a life.

The French Girl at Work

You cannot divorce the French girl and her relationship to work from French life and its intractable relationship to bureaucracy. France is a society of *functionnaires*—bureaucrats who wield the power of paper the way colonialists wielded the power of the bayonet. This makes French working life somewhat black or white. (You are either part of the system or you are not.)

There's a certain wonderful and infuriating stasis in French life. Infuriating because the French have a sense of entitlement that comes from the generous (and in some cases overprotective) socialist underpinnings of the French government, which assures the French a thirty-five-hour work week, five weeks of vacation each year, numerous national holidays (which all, miraculously, seem to fall on a Monday or Friday) and makes them among the most spoiled nation in the industrialized world—of which the French seem blissfully unaware. Wonderful, on the other hand, because this very sense of entitlement lets them disassociate from work life in ways that are ultimately very healthy.

Forget irreverence for the gears that turn the wheels of customer relations. I've always been impressed with certain contradictions about the French girl and her compatriots when it comes to working life: Their trains arrive with Germanic precision all over the hexagon, pulling into forgotten little pre-war stations at the exact minute scheduled. They've launched space shuttles, run a good chunk of the country on nuclear power, and were the first to actually invent the microchip. And yet their thoroughly modern industriousness is tempered by a Latin emphasis on leisure and certain stubbornly antiquated notions, like the persistent trend among companies to use handwriting analysis to determine the character of job candidates, or the blessed capacity to kiss everything goodbye—that pressing deadline, that letter that absolutely *must* go out the door this afternoon—for the pleasures of a three-course lunch.

The lack of a workaholic culture, with all of its inherent dis-ease, takes the peculiarly Anglo-Saxon strain out of the workplace, and frees the French girl to have a more sanely irreverent relationship to her work life. The results

are apparent in a myriad of small but pervasive details: Unless she's about to enter the operating room to do brain surgery, she'll leave work behind for meals—and she certainly won't carry on a business conversation on her cell phone during her meal, straining her voice over the din of diners. (Gauche, gauche, gauche.)

She won't necessarily bend over backwards and jump through hoops of fire to meet an excessively tight deadline. (While freelancing in France, I worked with a designer who was so chronically late that countless critical details fell into black holes. "She's an artist," my French co-workers said by way of explanation with a shrug.) And she'll rarely smile effusively and tell you to "Have a great day!"

"You smile all the time," my friend Karine complained

Her Work Face

There are certain unspoken truths that inform the French girl's professional life.

First, it's about working together and respecting protocol, not about radicalizing or reinventing or reorganizing the workplace. (She's got her union for that.)

She takes time to quietly figure out the culture and tenor of her work environment—and then she settles into it. Over-directness or painful honesty or disgruntled complaints are not welcome.

Politeness and form are at a premium at work. In formal circles, business acquaintances are known as Madame or Monsieur, not Sally and Bob. And, of course, they are addressed as *vous*.

Business conversation is often strictly formal. Personal life details are not exchanged or revealed and there's little of the happy-faced, ice-breaking small talk you have in America. That said, when a business meeting is held in a restaurant, or when partnerships and collaborations are in the air, a long prelude to deal-making that excludes shop talk will often take place. It is understood that a certain fraternizing will happen over the first round of drinks (and sometimes the second, well into a meal), before getting down to real business. The French schmooze is a little like foreplay, and getting right to the point before a certain intellectual tête-à-tête is considered poor form among many professionals.

Continued on next page . . .

The French girl has her coterie of well-established colleague friends, but you won't often see her and a gaggle of work girlfriends kvetching and guffawing over margaritas after work. That's not just because "happy hour" doesn't exist in France; but because you'll rarely see a gaggle of French girls anywhere—they just don't travel in packs. If she needs to let off steam from the day, the French girl is more likely to mull over a glass of wine and a smoke, read a good novel, or get lost in a movie—by herself.

And one last point: The French girl will not tell you what her salary is, or how much she got for her raise. Talking openly about money is quasi-taboo for the French. They are tight-lipped and tight-fisted, and hypocritical in some respects. (The French *do* care about money; they just don't talk about it openly.) Sharing financial details is not only considered gauche, but private to the point of being nearly immodest. (Our Parisian neighbor Michel had to scan my husband's tax documents and send them to us via email one day when we were in the States. "I guess that makes us truly intimate now," Michel said. And indeed, it did.)

of me. "You're always telling people how fabulous and great things are; you're always telling them to have a nice day. We French don't really care if you have a nice day, so we don't say it." Another way of explaining that there's no false sincerity or unctuous good cheer lubricating the gears of working life in France (though at times a little unctuousness wouldn't hurt).

"We only do well the things we like doing."
COLETTE

The French girl's work ethic is Latin, not Protestant, and her time flows around the banks and shoals of what is personally relevant. In fact, time management barely exists as an actual term in her language. Ditto for the word "multi-tasking." When I tried with a certain guilty self-implication to explain the term 'multi-tasking,' French girlfriend Audrey scoffed with lusty derision. "Multi what?" she asked. "What's the point? Why in the world would you want to be all things to all people, and do it all at once?"

There is little place in the French way of life for the implications of multi-tasking or the furious list-making overachieving running-behind-the-eight-ball that characterizes American life. To the harried rush for climbing the next rung, many French shrug with that classic air of nonchalance and disdain. "Life is just too bloody short," they seem to be saying.

The French girl honors time. She gives everything in her life its natural due, whether it's work or her family or her interests. Which is why when it comes to work, there's a natural balance in her life.

You'll see the French working girl on the metro, her slim leather backpack against a dark, wool jacket, looking

Fabriqué en France

If you must restore the subtle muted shades of an eighteenth-century fresco. Or build a boat exactly as it was built four hundred years ago, down to the specificity of its ancient masts. Or make a cello in the same baroque fashion it was made in the seventeenth century, then you must go to France. Because this is where the artisan still has an exalted place in the world.

The French artisan will often labor in ways so far afield from today's machine-driven culture that she appears almost whimsical. She will only work with authentic materials and techniques passed down over the centuries—for that is the very intrinsic nature of her work. She will take great, liberal amounts of time in executing each detail—for each detail, cycle, or maneuver requires it. She will use many, if not all, of her senses (she must smell, hear, touch, taste)—for sensual experience is at the very core of her creation. And she will produce a unique, high-quality piece of work the likes of which cannot possibly be reproduced in exactly the same way, nor bring the same level of tactile pleasure—for that is the nature and beauty of things made by the human hand.

composed and pensive. She's walking briskly down a cobblestone street with her satchel thrown over her shoulder, on her way to a business meeting. She's immersed in a book during a café lunch break. She's busy but not bedraggled. She doesn't seem harried. She's got a full load—

a job, maybe a child or two, a husband, the works—but she still manages to come home, make a pit stop at her local shops, enjoy a drink, make and have dinner *en famille*. Miraculously, it all seems to fall into place. How does she do it?

Well, she's not fretting over articles in women's magazines that want to help her find ways to "do it all." She's not frantically trying to patch together some "quality time" with her family. And she's not raging against glass ceilings or sexual harassers or gender discriminators. This isn't to say everything is perfect for the French working girl—she faces distinct inequalities with men on pay, job responsibility, promotion and job security, just like the rest of us. But she does her work and lives her life, and she takes very French pains not to let one overtake the other.

She's also not burdened with a host of familiar icons: the super mom, the soccer mom, the over-burdened overachiever who's storming the boardroom with a guilty conscience about the family she's left behind. The French girl doesn't grow up with these archetypes and doesn't much admire them, either. Why? Perhaps it's because the media has not claimed its stake on her life with conflicting, guilt-inducing messages about motherhood. Or because her culture has long favored the pleasures of living life over the pressures of making a living. Maybe it's the long-standing Latin bias in France to disassociate (in ways that are pre-eminently sane) who you are with what you do for a living. Or the blood that's been spilt for hard-won

French Girls We Love

COCO CHANEL

For ivory slingbacks with black patent toes. For quilted hand-bags and gold chains. For turtleneck sweaters. For giving women permission to wear pants and "working" suits—and for sewing ribbons in the waists of those suits to keep the blouses from slipping. But mostly we love Coco Chanel for "the little black dress" and Chanel No. 5, two defining signature statements and enduring elements of French girl style. Chanel was an orphan, raised without means, but she is proof that a woman's place is wherever she wants it to be: "There is no time for cut-and-dried monotony. There is time for work. And time for love. That leaves no other time."

Read Janet Wallach's beautifully illustrated biography, *Chanel: Her Style and Her Life.*

workers' rights and affordable childcare. It could have to do with the fact that French men do things that would make many American men run for cover—like wear bi-kinis and, yes, change diapers. Or the fact that French society in general is so well-stocked with social benefits that the French girl feels taken care of in ways that we Americans could only dream of.

I've been a mother on both sides of the cultural divide. In France, I enjoyed the luxuries (to the French, they're basic human rights) of France's socialized healthcare sys-tem: Week-long post-maternity stays in French hospitals. Post-natal at-home care. A host of certified daycare specialists. Pediatricians who always make inexpensive house calls. Free high quality nursery schools and state-subsidized nannies when grandma wasn't around. I came to understand the deeply-rooted sense of comfort that the working French girl feels living in a society that does not pay lip service to family values but supports them in truly concrete, self-evident ways. In America, I revel in the vastness of options. But being a working mother in America is a little like standing on a precipice facing the wind: You have an incredible view, but if you're not careful, it can do you in.

L'Amour, Inc.

High-profile office romances have created a national peep show consciousness in the States, thanks in great measure to the American media. The reality is that boardroom dalliances have always existed all over the globe and the French happen to simply take it all in stride. The French girl enjoys the little perks of being a *femme* and accepts the inevitable workplace flirtations and seductions as part of basic human nature. She knows that under every workplace lies the inevitable groundswell of human emotion and desire. Put two members of the opposite sex in a room and there's bound to be some sexual vibe—good, bad or indifferent. And she's entirely comfortable with that. "We want to keep the freedom to be seduced—and to seduce," wrote French feminist Sylviane Agacinski, speaking of French girls everywhere.

"Jean is sleeping with Marie? Who cares, as long as they do their jobs correctly." This is how the French girl sees it. When the Clinton/Lewinsky affair exploded on the international scene, my favorite wine merchant leaned over his barrels of ruby vintage Bordeaux and asked in complete consternation, "We French expect our politicians to have an active sex life. How can they properly run the country without one?" So ingrained in the culture is sexual engagement, even at work.

The pursuit of life, liberty, and lots of cash has never been high on the French girl's agenda. If she's lucky, there's a happy resonance between who she is and what she does for a living. If she's blessed, she makes her living at her passion. But there's always an awareness that the most fulfilling aspect of what work has to offer is what work ultimately affords—which is the means to spend your hard-earned Euros doing exactly the opposite of work: namely, play.

Borrow a Page From the French Girl's Book: Work

Invest in your work life but strive for balance. Remember that work is something that you do, not who you are. Don't try to manage time; you can only manage what you choose to do with your time. Accept the natural human tendency to flirt and flatter. If an office romance blooms, let it tend to itself. But keep it to yourself, too.

Le Film

UN HOMME ET UNE FEMME
(A Man and a Woman)

This 1966 Claude Lelouch film with Anouk Aimée and Jean-Louis Trintignant is known as the quintessential French love story. It is also interesting to look at the almost documentary-type scenes of the man and the woman at work. Anouk Aimée's character is a script girl working in film production (he is a race car driver—hardly a nine-to-five job, but still) and their unconventional romance progresses against the backdrop of their highly charged professions. The way the woman approaches her job and her lover with equal amounts of passion is one of the things that makes this movie endure.

The French Girl at Play

Every other Sunday Claudie stops her life, packs a bag, grabs a wooden box filled with oil paints, and disappears to a friend's country home in Normandy to paint. On Saturday mornings, after trolling the quais for rare books, Nadine throws her stash in an old Deux-Chevaux and putts her way to her country home, where she toils in her tangled, flourishing vegetable garden—pruning, picking and plodding through squash leaves the size of dinner plates. And Frédérique will simply walk alone through the Tuileries, uninterrupted except for her own ruminations—

The French Girl's Work Uniform

It's not the cleavage of Erin Brockovich. But it's not the stiff suit of the sexless female exec, either. Yet femininity trumps powerdressing every time. The French girl wears elegant, well-made clothes. Her skirt might be close-fit and her heels might be high—and she may even have a hint of *décolletage* peeking from her silk blouse, or no stockings at all. There is far less conservatism in the way the French girl dresses for work, and no such thing as "casual Fridays" because unless she works for the military, she can be casual whenever she wants. But you won't see her walking to work in a Chanel suit and tennis shoes. And there's no question she's taken seriously—and even less of a question when it comes to her femininity. She's smartly put together; attractive but not distractingly alluring; in short, the picture of self-possession at work.

thinking, daydreaming and taking in the weather, no matter how inclement it might be.

The French girl luxuriates in her free time and fills it intelligently. The TV is hardly on and house-cleaning is rarely high on her nonexistent to-do list. She has museums to tour, galleries to visit, books to read, films to see, antiques to hunt, parks to stroll, gardens to grow, friends to meet and great, sumptuous meals to eat.

French Girls We Love

MARIE DE FRANCE

For being the first professional French woman writer . . . in the twelfth century! A native of Normandy, she earned her living by composing poems or "lays" for French royalty, including Henry II and Queen Eleanor. She was part of their collection of troubadours or *trouvères* and wrote little poem-songs about the brave deeds of knights in a sort of sing-for-your-supper fashion. Read her collection of 103 fables called *Ysopet*, the Breton cycle of lays, or a romance called *Legend of the Purgatory of Saint Patrick*.

Le Soir

The French girl spends her evenings on her interests and entertainments. She might cook for friends, go for cocktails with her beau, take in a film or hear some jazz in a tiny smoky club. At home for an evening alone, she'll cook a simple meal for herself, read, listen to music, maybe spend a little quality time on her body. Her evenings are carefully and meaningfully spent—she rarely plans her free time around the *TV Guide* or picks herself up from the couch after a long mind-numbing spell in front of the tube wondering what she did with her night.

Le Weekend

Before the French borrowed the word "weekend" from us to describe the much-needed interlude between work weeks, they called it *fin de semaine* (end of the week). As with her evenings, when she turns her attention from work to weekend, she does it completely. She gardens, she antiques, she overnights with friends. She throws a dinner party, she goes to the ballet, she takes long walks, she goes for a swim, she meets her family for Sunday lunch. There's a rhythm and pattern to her weekend that sanctifies leisure. This time is not to be squandered but invested in things of meaning and value and resonance. Her playtime can be light and lively and utterly spontaneous but at the same time it is usually rich and deep and connected with her culture and her history. Invariably, that means that the briefcase stays in the office, the cell phone is turned off, and the computer is at rest.

Le Jardin

A few years ago I went to a garden show in Paris that was positively packed with budding green thumbs and horticulturists of every shape and size. The French were in passionate pursuit of hoes, rakes, shovels, trowels, wheelbarrows, gloves and boots, not to mention seeds, gourds, planters, buds and blooms of innumerable plants.

The French girl has always loved her gardens, from the

Le Livre

THE CASTLE OF PICTURES AND OTHER STORIES: A GRANDMOTHER'S TALES
by George Sand

You may be familiar with the infamous nineteenth-century French novelist George Sand for her love affair with Chopin and her progressive thinking. But chances are you don't know this unusual book. She wrote *The Castle of Pictures and Other Stories: A Grandmother's Tale* "to educate as well as entertain her granddaughters." A wonderful guide for how to combine work and play, the fairy tales include "What do Flowers Say," "The Bug-Eyed Fairy," and "The Talking Oak." They describe creative, hardworking children meandering in fields, near rivers and woods, all the while discovering and learning about wildlife and culture. Here is a snippet from "What Flowers Say":

"I crept along in the shadow of the bushy hedge, heading toward the meadow. I wanted to know if the spirea, who are called queen of the meadow, were also proud and jealous. But I stopped next to a tall rosebush where the flowers were all talking to one another. 'Let's try to find out,' I was thinking, 'if the wild rose makes fun of the cabbage rose with a hundred petals and scorns the button rose.' "

With its tales of science and magic, the book still appeals to today's French Girl who uses ingenuity to offset boredom.

Sand lived and wrote in the idyllic village of Gargilesse, where many French artists have visited or lived. Her adult novels, as well as *The Castle of Pictures*, describe the surrounding area. Set in a valley with its own château, cafés, and hotels, it still makes an appealing vacation destination for modern pleasure seekers.

Feeling Good In Her Skin

There is a phrase, *bien dans sa peau*, which means "to feel good in one's skin." It is a state of mind to which the French aspire, a state of ease and contentment that they hope is reflected in their faces. No worry wrinkles, no cheeks flushed with stress. Being *bien dans sa peau* is a state of simple physical and emotional grace. You live well. You do not have a guilty conscience for personal pleasures. You feel good about yourself on a very essential level, and so others feel good around you. The French girl who is *bien dans sa peau* is balanced. Relaxed. Natural. At ease in body and soul. A perfect description of the French girl at her best.

rows of verdant horticulture landscaped with surgical precision in great civic spaces and châteaux to the wild, austere provincial gardens of blustery lavender and rosemary, or the countless courtyards where a theatrical display of lovingly tended bloom creates absolute beauty and charm.

Germaine Greer once said of Colette: "No one has written better about gardens than Colette. Her mother, Sido, gardened passionately above and below their house at Saint-Sauveur-en-Puisaye. Colette, her youngest child, was left to moon and dawdle around the plants as much as she liked. Plants were her earliest and most faithful companions; she looked into them as deep and hard as

> "The deeper the civilization of a country may to a great extent be measured by the care she gives to her flower garden—the corner of her life where the supposedly 'useless' arts and graces flourish. In the cultivating of that garden France has surpassed all modern nations; and one of the greatest of America's opportunities is to find out why."
>
> EDITH WHARTON

only a child can, and she never forgot what she learned. Of each she remembered the mode and the imprint, as well as the way it behaved in garden society. The gardens she liked least were the ones she herself had to make from scratch; she entered fully into the atmosphere of gardens already existing, complete with their animals and insects. Each crumbling wall, with its rampant stragglers and tangled blooms attended by ragged butterflies, worked its way into her memory."

For the French girl, the garden is a microcosm of the world, a wild open space where the cycles of nature play out under her fingertips, bringing her persistent small pleasures on a daily basis.

French Girls We Love
ROSA BONHEUR

For being the most successful working girl among the artsy set of the nineteenth century. A painter, she started earning money by the time she was seventeen by copying paintings in the Louvre. Eventually, her own work hung there, as well as in the Metropolitan Museum of Art in New York. Bonheur flouted convention, wearing men's clothes for their practicality as she visited cattle markets, horse fairs, and dissected animals to learn anatomy in order to improve her art. That's what we call a French girl hard at work. Read Dore Ashton's *Rosa Bonheur: A Life and a Legend* and Anna Klumpke's *Rosa Bonheur: The Artist's (Auto) Biography*. See Bonheur's "The Horse Fair" at the Met.

Les Vacances

One of the best examples of the way the French value and experience their vacations involves not a French girl, but a French boy. Forty-something Laurent had never been to America. He'd studied it. He'd memorized long passages of Alexis de Tocqueville's *Democracy in America*, wept while watching *The Shop Around the Corner*, and had ferocious opinions about almost every American president. One day when I was in Los Angeles for a summer vacation, the phone rang. "J'arrive," Laurent said. Two days later, he was in California.

You can take the French boy out of France, but you can't take France out of . . . we know. A tall, lanky, French intellectual who hadn't seen a ray of sun in months, Laurent walked around in bikini underwear, prepared exquisite meals from produce he bought at local farmer's markets, read Proust on public beaches and flirted with local Latinas—among others. He studied with anthropological curiosity the *engouements* (read: fervent passions, enthusiasms) of Americans at street fairs and shopping malls. He rented a convertible Cadillac and drove alone, with a sense of delicious freedom in his own solace, through the stunning landscapes of the Southwest. Back from his road trip, the most critical imperative loomed ahead: to learn to surf. Wearing thick glasses and a thimble-sized Speedo, Laurent hired a Malibu surf jock to paddle through the waves off the Santa Monica bay and teach him to hang ten (which he did, with remarkable ease). "What does it mean, 'gnarly'?" Laurent yelled over the roar of the waves, flailing his arms as he straddled his board.

Back in France, Laurent's California furlough became a mythic memory. "I am saving my Euros," he said from his design studio in Paris, "to return to California. I miss the feeling of freedom there. And I am forgetting what it feels like to ride a wave."

Vacations in France are unbelievably long by Anglo-Saxon standard. They are also the cornerstone around which the entire French year seems to swing, and create great waves of migrating Europeans criss-crossing the country at roughly the same time. And they are an unbridled celebration of the pure pleasure of simple (and simply) living. The French girl's vacation often involves long, drowsy days doing close to nothing, or similarly long, drowsy days doing one or two small things over and over again—like reading, making meals, swimming, baking bread.

There is an old country home in almost every French girl's life, a place passed down from one ancestor to another where she spent nearly every summer as a child, imbibing the rural pleasures of provincial life and the requisite lazy boredom that is not only inevitable but a necessary part of childhood reverie. Later, providence, a taste for the exotic and curiosity about the world will take her not only throughout her own country but to the shores of post-colonial North Africa, across the Atlantic to America, further still to Tahiti (a destination for daily planeloads of French vacationers), or Australia. The French girl might wander to the farthest flung corners of the planet, but she'll inevitably, invariably, return to France.

Compared to Americans, the French have so much leisure time at their disposal one wonders how they get everything accomplished. In fact, they don't (and they're fine that way, *merci beaucoup*). A look at French work and play time:

- Everyone from businessmen to bus drivers gets four or five weeks of paid vacation each year. That's *every* year. (And *everyone* takes this vacation.) No I'm-too-busy-to-take-a-vacation martyrs.

Le Livre

BONJOUR TRISTESSE
by Françoise Sagan

Sagan's first novel was published in 1954 when she was a mere nineteen. Her main character, Cécile, is a seventeen-year-old used to having her widowed father all to herself. Cécile's carefree idyll in the world of the rich and beautiful comes to an end, of course, but not until we get to savor that world vicariously. Read it for descriptions of summer holidays spent at a villa in the south of France, replete with exquisite moments of eating an orange in the sun and swimming in the sea. And then rent the video of the Otto Preminger film starring David Niven, Deborah Kerr, and Jean Seberg. Although the Parisian scenes are shot in black and white, the Riviera is portrayed in all its Technicolor splendor.

- In addition to its generous allotment of vacation time, France enjoys numerous official national holidays, saints days and three-day weekends.
- The average French dinner lasts 1 ½ hours. The family does not eat in shifts to accommodate little Jacques' soccer practice. And it does not rush through a meal so as not to miss an episode of *Les Simpsons*.
- French commerce still closes for lunch. Some shops close for up to three hours. Inconvenient if you absolutely must have a pound of Roquefort at 2:00 P.M.? Yes. More human? Certainly.

Favorite French Girl Vacation Destinations

Alps, Val d'Isère: ski, snow, total physical abandon in winter.

Brittany, Belle-Île: nautical, blustery, picking mussels at low tide, eating oysters, boats, roaming foggy beaches in thick wool sweaters and heavy boots.

Venice: Romantic, sultry, moody, sensual. In winter, the carnaval!

Rome: Ditto Venice (with lots of art thrown in).

New York: Skyscrapers, urban density, the gigantic bustling spirit of America.

California & the Southwest: Hollywood, beaches, sun, deserts, road trips down empty highways, the glamour myth of America.

Morocco: Cheap post-colonial resorts, exotic shopping at the Casbah, a quick plane ride across the Mediterranean for much-needed winter sun.

Aix-en-Provence: For fields of lavender, Roman ruins, and *soupe au pistou*.

French West Indies (St. Bart): Same reason as Morocco, only tropical, with pina-coladas and snorkels.

A tiny secret village in Ardèche, the Cantal, Dordogne or the Luberon where there are no tourists, no brand outlets, no cinémathèque. This place is her little secret, her family hideaway, her lonesome, winsome country heaven where she returns throughout her life on a regular pilgrimage.

> "People who know how to employ themselves always find leisure moments, while those who do nothing are forever in a hurry."
>
> MARIE JEANNE ROLAND

- While controversial, French law mandates a thirty-five-hour work week. This makes room in every day for those long lunches and long, late dinners. And leaves the French in a state of deep contentment.

Fin

The French girl's perception of work and play is inextricably woven into the structure of her culture, with its built-in social protections and an irrepressible commitment to lei-

Borrow a Page from the French Girl's Book: Leisure

Take off your watch. Turn off the computer. Ditch the cell phone. Read, ride your bike, stroll, paint, bake bread, be with your kids, grow your garden, luxuriate in the art of doing absolutely nothing. Observe your own day of rest with religious conviction. Lounge, loll, unbuckle your belt, go on furlough.

What the French Girl Loves about Us

American literature

Cheerful goodwill and down-home hospitality

A certain naiveté

Kitsch

Cosmetics (Mac, Bobby Brown, Clinique)

Basic functional clothes (Levi's, Calvin Klein, Gap)

Elvis and Jerry (Lewis, of course); Pop music

Big open spaces

The hipness of health

Classic Hollywood cinema and road movies (not mainstream blockbusters)

The taste for risk taking and novelty; the lack of certain conventions

The ability to work well into your seventies, as long as you love what you do

General garden-variety American eccentricity

sure; a culture defined by England to the north, Germany to the east, and Spain and Italy to the south. With this particular blend of Anglo-Saxon, Germanic, and Latin sensibilities, her mindset is shaped by the winds sweeping off these cultural vistas, but more fundamentally by the wisdom of the very French Voltaire. Among other sage counsel he appealed to the French to cultivate their gardens. The metaphor was not lost on these pleasure-loving people, and so despite all the challenges of these modern times, they work hard but still find time to smell the roses.

Conclusion

I'm now split between two countries: France and America. I spent my last day in Paris, before the big move to California, with my friend Chantal. As we strolled past the luxuries of St. Honoré (Chloé, Lanvin) and the sugar-coated fruit jellies and huge tins of fragrant bulk tea at Hediard, Chantal summed up French girlishness in all her particular tastes and inclinations.

She bought a bustier by Jean-Paul Gaultier at his *prêt-à-porter* boutique and a peasant skirt from Tati, the discount bazaar filled with boxes of ten-franc scarves. She picked out a rare book on botanics at La Maison Rustique and sheaves of transparent writing paper from Calligrane (a dreamy little stationery store for hard-core paper and pen aficionados). She handpicked glass buttons for a shirt at a haberdashery (". . . it's for this little white blouse I have," she said) and a vintage man's tie to go with a simple white blouse. She ate delicious round cakes from the Gérard Mulot *patisserie* and seriously thick *cassoulet* from Chez Camille. And instead of the well-trodden favorites, Chantal took us to the eccentric Musée de la Serrure (the lock museum) to admire ancient Roman door knockers and the original handmade lock to Marie Antoinette's apartment. At the Musée de l'Histoire de France, she sought out the letters of Voltaire and Joan of Arc.

That day with Chantal comes up often in memory: The way she ate without a moment's hesitation, licking the little flakes of *mille-feuille* from her fingers with guiltless pleasure. The way she shopped with discrimination, but not necessarily obsessed with practicality. Despite her love for a good fight (like many French girls she has ferocious opinions about things) she was also comfortable with silence, looking out at the busy crowds as we ate, taking in their faces, lost in thought.

There is clearly something to say about coming from a

mythic country, whose major city is a mecca of good taste, high culture, and haute couture. Like her country the French girl is not striving to become; she just *is*. We, on the other hand, like our own country, are still in the process of becoming. Where French girl seeks culture or knowledge, we seek self-improvement, self-help. This is our burden and our blessing. It makes us open to novelty and the unknown, but also unsure of who we are.

In many ways, the archetypal French girl is a counterpoint to our world. She's a sensualist and a libertarian. She's a giver, but she doesn't give herself away. She's not a worrier. Her consciousness is very likely rooted in the historical underpinnings of the world around her, even as she embraces the future, thoroughly modern.

To unleash her, we don't have to act French or (God forbid) pretend to be French. But we might want to rethink our values. Reject certain aspects of the status quo. Reposition ourselves against the currents (raging at times) that pull us away from our own center.

Edith Wharton reminds us that "the four words that preponderate in French speech and literature are: Glory, love, voluptuousness, and pleasure." Add to that list self-possession, discretion, authenticity and sensuality, and you're well on your way to finding your inner French girl. *Bon voyage.*

Acknowledgments FOR DEBRA OLLIVIER

The inner French girl owes her existence to individuals on both sides of the Atlantic.

To my American contingent, many heartfelt thanks to honorary French girl Laurie Wagner, for her generosity of spirit and literary talents. To Pauline Ores, for her insightful words of wisdom in the early phases of the book's life. And to Lori Staff, for her astute reading of the manuscript in its various forms. Many heartfelt thanks as well to Karen Watts and her colleagues at Lark Productions, for their collaboration and contributions; and to Elizabeth Beier at St. Martin's Press, for her French girl enthusiasm and editorial savoir-faire.

Across the Atlantic, special enduring gratitude to Frédérique La Fonta, Henri Houssay, and to my husband's family, who opened the door to a world beyond the "fortress that is Paris."

For over ten years I enjoyed, on an almost daily basis, the bountiful cooking, humor, resilient good spirits, and tremendous warmth of Martine Tramus. Her two lovely daughters, Elisa and Eléanore, and her husband, Michel *le docteur*, were also an essential part of my life in France. They have all offered me keys to the ways and wisdom of the inner French girl.

Finally, to my mother, who gave me a sense of freedom and a ticket to Paris. To my husband, without whom France would not be my adopted country. And to our two children, both of whom rooted me in the bedrock of French life in ways that only children can.

Acknowledgments FOR LARK PRODUCTIONS

Sometimes it takes un village to make a book. Lark Productions would like to acknowledge the skill and energy and creativity that is always required to bring a great idea to life. We would like to applaud the spirit and talent Debra Ollivier brought to this project. We're exceedingly grateful to our editor,

Elizabeth Beier, for her wonderful affection for our subject, her wisdom, and her good humor. And we thank Joanne Heyman for her enthusiasm and insight, which always came at the right time.